GATLINBURG LIGHTS

by

DONNA LEA

Gatlinburg Lights

Foothills Patchworks Press
Maryville, TN

Printed by Patterson Printing
Benton Harbor, Michigan

Cover by Rhonda Swicegood of Hart Graphics
Knoxville, Tennessee

Library of Congress Catalog Number 97-90365
ISBN 0-9658084-3-2

DEDICATION

There are so many people I love in this world. My children, family and friends mean so much to me. But I will dedicate this book to the loved ones who started it all.

Mom,
I dedicate this book to you for all the times you told me I had a vivid imagination. You light up my life, even though now it's with a heavenly glow. Please keep watch over me as I wander closer through this world.

And Dad,
You taught me humor, patience and a love of reading. What could I do but try to put it all into words? Just close your eyes when you read certain parts, okay?

My heartfelt thanks also go out to all of the professionals who have helped me so much in this endeavor.

As always, it started with the mountains. Their siren song haunted her and became a part of her soul. The blue haze of their air penetrated her heart and permeated her skin to the very center of her being. Their pine softened peaks murmured her name in every wind, bringing homesickness for a place never called home. Southern breezes of spring sought pledges of her return. Storm-racked skies recalled memories of their echoes, mountainside to mountainside to mountainside.

She envisioned the open fields suddenly stretching themselves to new heights, no longer pasture for anything but lopsided cattle. And beyond to land only suited for nimble footed or winged beasts. How she longed to stand at the top of this world, surveying the lower ranges and gazing on snow covered peaks while valleys below grew warm with winter sunshine. Where hawks circled endlessly through mountain passes, swooping, curling, watching, waiting. While land sloped gently to catch water in red clay-rimmed highland lakes; rivers that had lost their independence to earthen and concrete dams. Where invisible night-blackened mountains braced lights that seemed to glimmer from the middle of nowhere.

How she loved the serene old mountain women, their wrinkled faces miming the truths of their lives. And the sun-parched old men who toiled in dry tobacco patches, praying ancient prayers for a gentle rain.

She yearned to hear mountain silences, still as sleeping babies. Or the racket of rain swollen rivers pounding like kettle drums over boulders too large to have been placed by anyone less than God. To see a hundred named and nameless places. Places like LeConte, Silers Bald, and Juney Whank Falls all complaining silently, yet insistently at her neglect. To drive on roads climbing and winding higher and higher, always trying to span that one last ridge, that one last curve, that one last glimpse of the sunset until their narrow paths evaporated into nothingness.

And always, from their granite cores, promises. Promises too strong to be denied yet too silent to be ignored. Promises as yet undeclared. But promises, all the same. Promises to be kept and needs to be met.

PART

ONE

Chapter 1

"Kelsie? Kelsie, are you asleep?" Samantha whispered, quietly enough to not risk waking the young girl stretched out on the bed. Luckily there was no response.

She threw on her comfortable old sweatshirt and favorite jeans then wrote a quick note.

"Tried to wake you. Gone to town. Back in a bit. Wait for me!!! Love ya, Mommy Dearest."

Propping it on the television, she noiselessly backed out the door. Gatlinburg lay at the bottom of the hill, waiting like a long lost friend.

She tried not to think about Kelsie's wet-hornet mood she would have to face later. Being left behind would not sit well with her sixteen-year-old daughter.

Once outside she forgot all about Kelsie and anger. She lifted her face and raised her arms, embracing the weak late fall sunshine with every inch of her body. The fiery hues of fall on the mountains behind the Bon Aire Motel had been replaced by a more somber cast of winter-ready gray. Only the pines retained their ever-present green, but she would have had to disagree if someone had told her they were drab.

The chocolaty aroma of fudge drifted up from Aunt Mahalia's Candy Shop. Samantha inhaled deeply and ambled as slowly as possible down the steep driveway, letting her nose lead the way into the store. After she toured the town she would buy some chocolate-peanut butter fudge as a peace offering for Kelsie. For now she bought a quarter pound bag of 2" jelly beans, the biggest and best she had ever tasted. She bit the end off a green one and stuffed the bag in her sweatshirt pocket, open and easily accessible from the side.

Standing in front of the store, she looked up and down the Parkway. The nearest end led to the Great Smoky Mountain National Park. First thing tomorrow she would head there, dragging Kelsie to Cade's Cove for the day. Or maybe she'd let Kelsie talk her into crossing the mountains to Cherokee.

The main part of town was to her right, and unaware that she had a choice in the matter, she turned that way. That direction held most of the shops and the majority of the three million lights that were unlit in the bright afternoon sunshine.

Alabama's "Christmas in Dixie" was quietly being piped through loudspeakers attached to light posts. Its words "snowing in the pines" brought a deep and desperate melancholy she could never quite explain, even to herself.

The large window display of one shop was covered with angel hair and a glazed ceramic village. Samantha almost ignored it, thinking it was yet another display of a Department 56 Christmas town. But a miniature, perfectly proportioned Space Needle caught her eye. It was then that she realized the Lilliputian village copied much of the city of Gatlinburg. Live boughs of short needle pines around the edges gave the impression of evergreens wrapping the village in warmth and security, much as the trees surrounding the town actually did. Pinpricks of light draped from light post to light post. The tiny stoplights were even numbered like their larger counterparts hanging above the road behind her. She glanced at the real stoplight Number 7 and saw identical decorations. Even their red and green globes seemed to add to the "Merry Christmas" atmosphere. The only thing lacking from the real scene was the layer of snow the angel hair represented and she almost missed its brightness. Squinting through the glass, she was able to read the discrete price tag that lay in the corner. It read "Gatlinburg Village, $3,500. Pieces available separately. Inquire within."

"Yeah, right," she muttered to no one as she strolled on.

Samantha watched the people in the crowds as they wove their own little web worlds; young parents catching up to small children, grown children holding on to aged parents, lovers entwined, cautiously or not, with arms around each other's waists. Most were smiling and laughing, joking with their friends and families about all of the money they were saving and spending. Samantha watched husbands as they followed their wives from shop to shop. Few complained aloud although some raised their eyes to the heavens as soon as their wives walked through the door of yet another store.

"Come on honey, we'd better get moving. We've still got ninety-nine shops to go," she overheard one husband say and she smiled at his weary, yet good-natured tone.

She watched the lovers least of all. It had somehow slipped her mind that Gatlinburg claimed to be the "Honeymoon Capital of the South". Being a single woman in the midst of a couples' paradise caused her to slow her steps for a few seconds. She watched them holding hands, kissing and sweet-talking in the way of lovers everywhere. That part of her life was but a hazy memory. Sometimes she wanted to be a soul mate more than anything in the world. But only sometimes. Most days her independent lifestyle suited her fine.

The festivity in the air let her forget, for the moment, what was lacking in her life. Everyone was celebrating Christmas even though it was only the middle of November. Christmas came early in this part of the Smoky Mountains, if only for the sake of the tourists and the dollars they would spend.

Samantha walked slowly past dozens of shops. Window shopping, she reminded herself as she longingly gazed at the stained glass angels hanging on suction cup hooks. They had turned in $200 worth of quarters, dimes, nickels and pennies as well as the last of her stash of traveler's checks to get here. This trip was their Christmas present to each other, an escape hatch from the reality of winter that was so rapidly closing in on Lansing, Michigan, their home town.

She hesitated at a display window filled with Santas, noticing the all too perfect faces, the assembly line clothes and the $200 price tags. At least the Santas she made had character, each face showing a totally distinct personality. Her Santas' clothes were painstakingly different, showing off the mood, soul and heredity of the wearer. Besides, hers were hand-crafted, not made in China as these probably were.

She pulled a small notebook out of her pocket and wrote down the name of the shop, planning to come back here tomorrow and bring her sample. At the last minute she had stuck her fanciest Santa in the trunk of her car thinking she might drum up some orders for next year. Maybe this was just the boost her blooming business and low bank account needed.

She stopped again at the entrance to the Mountain Mall. It sat in the "Y" of the main downtown streets and held five half-stories of jewelry, crafts and art. Especially art, Samantha thought as she pulled open the door and headed up the stairs, ignoring for now the shops at the top of each landing.

Chapter 2

"Prestige Prints", the art gallery on the top level, was always her first stop. Once there, she no longer cared about the outside world. She could spend hours looking at how local artists portrayed the mountains that were clearly visible from almost any vantage point in town. Lee Roberson's "Home By Dark" print number 767/1000 hung in her living room, always making her wish she was fixing supper in that mountain home instead of in her big city house so far away from cabins, mountains and the peace they brought her.

That painting was part of her divorce settlement and the way her life was going, she would never be able to buy another print, not to mention the small secluded mountain cottage she'd hoped for. Her teacher's salary paid for the necessities, but since the two of them had moved out on their own two years ago, luxuries like art and steak dinners had been replaced by lawn mower repairs and Taco Bell.

"Oh well, it's worth it," she reminded herself, not realizing she had spoken aloud until a man sitting at a table across the room turned his head to stare at her.

"Talking to myself as usual," she told him, embarrassment marking her cheeks. He smiled without much interest then turned back to whatever lay on the table before him.

Slowly, trying to keep her curiosity from being obvious, she wandered around the store. She noticed the works of an artist she hadn't seen before, the scrawl of his signature impossible to make out. These paintings seemed to speak to her of the things she loved most about these mountains; old farmsteads sighted in green valleys, spring dogwoods blooming profusely in mountain woodlands, a single bluebird perched precariously on a much used, tilted wheelbarrow. She picked out the one she would buy if she happened to find a winning lottery ticket floating in the Little Pigeon River. The pink-purple of the redbud blossoms around a weather-beaten ancient barn could have brought a feeling of spring even when the bitter winds of February blew its icy pellets against her windows.

Finally, after slowly and nonchalantly making the full round of the shop, she stood behind the man. Her breath snagged in her throat as she looked over his shoulder. On the heavy watercolor paper in front of him a small clearing was surrounded by tall wispy pines, their branches appearing to blow silently in a wintery breeze. Mountain peaks filled the not too distant background and early morning hoarfrost coated the entire scene like a thick layer of bleached cotton batting. An old gnarled apple tree stood off to one side of the clearing, its brown-tinged apples clearly past their prime. All of this combined to bring a sudden serenity to Samantha; total, complete and unexpected.

The man felt her presence and turned to her inquiringly.

"Can I help you, ma'am?" he asked, his gentle Southern drawl stretching the words to captivating lengths.

The spell was broken and she surprised herself by asking softly, "Would it bother you if I watch for a while?"

Conrad turned sideways to get a better look at his visitor, the one he had heard talking to herself earlier. He was used to women hitting on him. On long, hot, muggy summer afternoons he sometimes watched cautiously as they ambled around the store, taking much longer than was necessary. They examined each and every picture as if they seriously intended to purchase it. Eventually their husbands got bored and would announce angrily that they were going across the street for an iced tea or a beer. The women would mutter a derogatory word or two. Then, when their hubby was safely out of sight, they made their moves. Some did no more than straightforward flirting, others hit on him so hard he was glad that Lucile, the shop owner, was somewhere nearby. More than once she had rescued him from an overtly-amorous admirer, of his work he tried to assume. Or maybe they associated danger with middle-aged small town artist types bearing shaggy graying beards and multicolored, paint-stained bluejeans. Conrad smiled secretly at that thought. He was about as dangerous as a caterpillar, but he wasn't about to tell them that.

Sometimes, when things were slow, he offered just enough of himself to get the women to buy. He knew they would show off his painting to their friends while making up stories about the artist who couldn't keep his eyes off them. He got a lot of repeat business from these women and the friends they sent his way. And it cost him nothing but a little bit of his pride.

Puts food on the table he told himself, bringing his attention back to the woman standing patiently beside him. She looked relatively harmless. There didn't seem to be a husband around. Nor was there the indentation of a pocketed wedding ring on the left hand that she used to push her hair back from her face. Besides, the eyes looked more fatigued than flirtatious, though they did have a certain sparkle that he somehow found kind of attractive.

"No problem," he said smiling warmly before returning to work. He watched her out of the corner of his eye for a long moment, then focused his attention back to the brush in his fingertips.

He couldn't believe his eyes when a minute later Lucile brought up a high stool and placed it off to his left side. Lucile, who generally chased the women away, was actually egging this one on. She ignored his dumbfounded look as she busied herself with a display near the door.

Samantha called out her thanks then hiked herself up on the round cushion. While her gray-blue eyes seemed intent on his painting, her thoughts wandered to the way he had smiled. Not the conceited one she had expected but a warm, inviting, welcome-to-my-world smile that would make any woman want to stay forever under its radiant heat. The best part was that he honestly didn't seem to realize how it affected and mesmerized her.

Rubbing her hands briskly over her knees to try to stop their quivering, she shook silly thoughts from her head and settled in to watch him. She often thought this stroke must certainly be his last, that the picture was flawless as it was and any more would only detract from its magnetism. But instead, as he continued to almost lovingly stroke the canvas, each mark made it more perfect somehow. She watched as the forest came alive with glittering white frost on the branches of the pines and brilliant sunlight streaking through to the frozen earth. Soon she forgot all about the mental image of him stroking her with the same tenderness and fell heart first into his painting.

Finally, Conrad leaned back in his chair, sighing in gratification. He frowned heavily at the painting. Today he wasn't sure if it was any good. Tomorrow he'd like it better. By the end of the week he would know it was good enough to sell. It worked that way for each and every one he had ever done.

"Wow," Samantha said after a few seconds. She stretched her feet to the floor and stood stiffly in front of the stool, her eyes drifting shyly from the painting to the painter.

Conrad jumped at the sound of her voice, glad his brush was inches above the canvas. She had been so quiet he had forgotten she was there. Tourists usually seemed bent on interrupting and their voices, if not their hands, would interfere with his concentration. But this one had sat without saying a word or moving a muscle for...he looked at his watch...an hour and a half.

He watched her stretch, a long cat-like movement that pulled the band of her sweatshirt up above her jeans and bared an inch of her stomach. That patch of skin sent a quick shudder of desire through his body, warning him like nothing else that he really needed to get out more often. He stared at her hard and long, noticing for the first time that her hair looked as if salt and pepper shakers had been spilled almost evenly over the strands, one silvery white, the next nearly black. He asked himself why this seemed to have the effect of an aphrodisiac as he took in the soft, middle-aged curves of her body.

Samantha turned away from the painting and looked into his eyes. Caught in lustful deliberation, Conrad coughed into his hand.

"I'm not a real fan of winter," he said trying to distract her gaze from the conspicuous reddening of his neck, "but it does make for a right pretty picture, doesn't it?"

"Yeah, if it wasn't slippery, cold, wet and a terror to drive in it would be a great season." Samantha braced herself, hoping her remark would bring that incredible smile back to his face. Instead she saw a flicker of intense pain but he covered this up more quickly than he had the blush.

"Yeah. Well, if pigs could fly..." Conrad looked deep into her eyes, trying to decipher how much of his grief she had seen.

"Exactly." Samantha squirmed at the intense scrutiny he seemed to be putting her soul through.

They both turned to the painting, unsure of what should come next.

"I really like this," Samantha said after a long, uncomfortable minute. "How much do you want for it?" She kept her eyes locked on the spoiling apples, having no idea where she would come up with the money. But she needed it to remind her of this magic moment in the artist's presence. So what if she had to give up eating until it was paid for. "It'd be perfect in my living room."

At first Conrad thought he must have misread the signals coming from her and was taken back by her tactlessness. Maybe she was, after all, one of those spoiled rich women who thought they could buy him along with his work. He looked more closely at the way she was dressed, seeing for the first time the frayed cuffs and washed out letters on her faded Gatlinburg sweatshirt. The purples and oranges of sunset were muted now, not the vibrant tones they had started off being. That and her scuffed, well worn tennis shoes showed that she was obviously anything but spoiled or rich. There was no way she could afford the $750 price tag he'd be able to hang on this and no way he could afford to take less. His mind wandered from the mouths he had to feed to the hesitant smile on the mouth in front of him.

"It's promised. I'm sorry," he said simply.

"Oh...well, I guess that's good," she said half a second later. "I was getting kinda fond of eating anyway. It's such a fantastic painting, though. I don't know how you managed to make it so...so perfect. Your trees look so real, your apples so spoiled, your frost so cold, your..." Suddenly Samantha clamped her mouth shut. She was babbling like a springtime mountain brook. "Sorry. Sometimes I talk too much."

Conrad grinned at her confession. "Hey, I'm not about to stop you. I'll keep listening as long as you keep complimenting. I really am sorry I can't sell it to you, but a promise is a promise." He truly hoped she wouldn't catch him in the little white lie that he could only insist was for her own good. Besides, what had she said about eating?

From across the room Lucile caught his eye. She pointed at her watch and to the door. The message was loud and clear.

"Geez, it's five already? We'd better get out of here before ornery old Lucile locks us in," Conrad said, smiling at Lucile's chagrin as he dipped his brush in black paint. He scrawled a signature across a dry area at the bottom then grabbed the old, worn-out *Highwaymen in Concert* t-shirt from a nail at the edge of the board.

"Must be the signature on those prints over there belongs to you. I couldn't make out what it said, but I knew I hadn't seen it before."

"Yeah, well, that chicken scratch adds to my mystique." He smiled again and Samantha melted a little more.

Her mind gradually shifted to Kelsie. Surely she was awake by now, likely to have grown impatient and taken off looking for her. Heaven only knew where she would be by now.

"Yeah, I've got to get back too," she said watching his hands gently pull the paintbrushes through the soft old T-shirt.

"Will your husband know where to find you once the shop closes?" Conrad asked, not knowing why he was praying she would give the right answer.

Samantha grinned at his question within a question. "My *husband* didn't try very hard to find me when we were married, so I doubt very much if he'd try now that we're divorced."

"Well, then can I walk with you?"

"Won't your wife wonder what's keeping you?" Samantha asked, deciding to make sure she had things straight. She'd found out the hard way that many men didn't wear rings.

"My *wife* couldn't be bothered to wonder about me when we were married, so I doubt very much if she would now."

Usually about this time he became tongue-tied but for some reason he felt comfortable with this woman. He grabbed his worn brown leather jacket off the hook in the supply room and flung it over his shoulder.

"Lucile, I'm outta here. See you Monday. Don't let those grandkids of yours fingerpaint on my picture."

When Lucile flicked the lights off behind them, Conrad touched Samantha's shoulder.

"Just a second."

Samantha watched him as he walked across the dusky room to look one more time at the work laying on the table. His head nodded slightly, seeming to accept that his painting was still a painting in the dim light. Samantha smiled at Lucile who beamed in obvious pride.

"Just checking," he said as he came back across the room. He held the door open and stepped aside while Samantha passed through. When Lucile came up behind him to lock the door, she grinned a large, knowing grin and flashed him a thumbs-up sign. Conrad scowled intently back at her then raised an arm in affectionate farewell.

Chapter 3

They stepped out of the mall and into the cool, early evening dusk. Fog cascaded over the city, making Samantha's vision seem blurry and unfocused. She wasn't sure if it was really the fog or part of her reaction to the dream world she seemed to be floating in. Shuddering as the dampness invaded her body, she wished she had thrown on her jacket before leaving the motel this afternoon.

"Here," Conrad said as he slipped his coat around her shoulders. It started to slide and he adjusted it to her much smaller frame letting his hand linger on her shoulder for only the briefest of extra seconds.

Samantha knew she should force him to take the coat back. His long sleeved T-shirt was covered only by a middle weight denim shirt and she knew he must be cold. But when he insisted she gave in easily, selfishly allowing herself to enjoy the pleasure of his scent. She resisted the urge to turn her head and snuggle her nose into the aftershave-scented leather, recognizing the "Canoe" her big brother had worn in high school. It had been a long time since she'd been in the company of a good smelling man...or a even a bad smelling one for that matter. She giggled quietly at her thoughts.

Conrad looked at her, wondering what was going on behind those baby blue eyes of hers. A smile slipped across his lips and Samantha's face lit up when his eyes met hers.

They walked slowly, the fog giving them a feeling of isolation from the hustle and bustle of the crowds around them. Part of

Samantha felt she should hurry back to Kelsie, but just this once she gave into the feelings of the moment. In her heart she knew Kelsie was fine and wouldn't do anything more foolish than swiping a couple of bucks from Samantha's purse and going for something to eat. Besides, Kelsie knew how her mom could dawdle when she got into that art store. But how would she feel if she found out that Samantha was dragging her feet so she could be with this man for a few minutes more?

"Jellybean?" she asked when she tried to stick her cold hands in her sweatshirt pocket and found the sack blocking the way. She handed him the crumpled bag and he picked out one, examining it carefully before biting off its black end.

"Where did you get these? They're huge."

"From Aunt Mahalia's Sweet Shop. You work upstairs from one and didn't know they had them?"

"Nah. Seems like I go into the shop, put in a few hours and then head home. Like most of us locals, I don't hit the tourists places much. I'll have to bug Claudine about these though. She knows I'm a jellybean freak. I woulda thought she'd have brought me some."

"She's had them for three or four years at least. I get them every time I'm here."

"Is that often? I mean, that you're here."

"I try to get down at least once a year. Twice sometimes, before the divorce. This past year or two it's only been for long weekends. A teacher's salary doesn't go very far when you're making house payments and paying bills."

"Teacher, huh. What grade?"

"Third."

"Good age."

"Yeah, I decided I like that age best. They still want to please and they're so curious about everything. My class this year is one of the best ever. We've got conferences next week so they gave everybody an extra couple of days off to get ready."

"Oh, playing hooky, huh?" he asked mischievously.

"No. I did my work early so I could come here instead."

"I'm glad you did."

Samantha stopped in the middle of the sidewalk. She stared at him for a long moment before she said, "Me too."

"Have you always lived in these mountains?" she asked after they had walked half a block in silence.

"Mostly, yes. Born and bred about ten miles out 321. Little place called Richardson's Cove."

"I envy you. Up in Michigan, where I'm from, about the only hills are the ones that are pushed up around the landfill. Do you realize how lucky you are to be able to wake up here, to see these mountains first thing when you walk out the door each morning and last thing before you go to bed at night?"

Conrad looked around at the mountains, now barely visible in the fog. "I didn't appreciate it 'til I left for a while back in the early seventies. We moved up to Nashville and I worked in a factory. Wasn't long before I decided the big city life wasn't for me, first week in fact. But my wife didn't agree so I stuck it out for seven years. Seven long, miserable years. Julia hated coming back, although she was from Sevierville. She finally left me about six years ago. Picked up her clothes and left, barely bothering to say goodbye to our two daughters."

"That must have been awful for your girls. How old were they?"

"Abby was seventeen and Lisa was eleven. We had some pretty rough times there for a while. I still can't think about Julia and those days without getting a little angry."

"I'm sorry." She walked on silently for a minute, trying to decide what to say next. "I guess David wasn't as obliging as Julia. I had to be the one to leave him after we'd been married for over twenty years. It was still tough on the kids. I tried to wait 'til they were grown, but I didn't make it. Jeff was older and had proposed to Jill but Kelsie was only fourteen. It was hardest on her. Still is for that matter."

"How long have you been divorced?"

"A little over two years. It's almost like asking someone how long they've been out on parole, isn't it?"

Conrad looped his arm around her shoulders and pulled her close for a brief hug. "It'll get easier, honest."

"You know, I'd never go back to that marriage even if I could, but being single isn't all it's cracked up to be either."

"Don't I know it. It took me better than three years just to realize I can get by without a woman around me all the time. I've finally learned that my worth isn't judged by whether or not I have a woman." Conrad took a few seconds before he added, "Not that I still wouldn't like to have somebody special."

"Me too," Samantha agreed quietly.

Silence descended again and Samantha was surprised at how comfortable it felt to be walking the streets of Gatlinburg with this stranger. Stranger! Here she was telling him her life history and she didn't even know his name. She opened her mouth to ask, but when she glanced his way, he seemed so deep in thought that she decided to keep still...for once.

Conrad's mind raced ahead while he tried to slow their pace to a crawl. In a few minutes he would deliver her to the door of her motel and that meant he was running out of time. He hadn't dated much since Julia took off, and the few times he had asked someone out he hadn't cared much what the answer would be.

Teenager's frustration seeped back into his mind like a long-drowsing monster. Thoughts of Pennie Jarnigan waltzed unbidden through his mind as he remembered having the worst crush in the world on her. They were in eighth grade when he'd embarrassed himself by asking his Mom to take them to the movies. She finally quit snickering and agreed to take them Friday night. Silently he prayed that she would be sober, hoping it wasn't asking too much.

He'd worked up the nerve to ask Pennie on Wednesday between fifth and sixth hour. Though his palms were sweaty and his knees were weak, he forced himself to stand between her and the doorway to her history class. His first word squawked as only a thirteen- year-old boy's voice could. Around him, everyone stopped and stared. He wanted to run and hide under the stairs until the halls were empty. But instead he stood his ground and asked his question. The blood rushed to his eardrums momentarily drowning out the sound of laughter coming from Pennie's mouth. Instead of "Why Conrad, I'd be honored," he heard, "Why, you greasy obese pig, I wouldn't go out with you if you were the last boy in all of Tennessee."

Conrad absentmindedly rested his hand on his now flat abdomen. He smiled to himself as he remembered the last time he'd seen Pennie. She weighed about 220 pounds, and her bleached blond hair was getting thin on the top. He'd heard that her husband knocked her around but he wasn't a good enough Christian to feel a whole lot sorry for her.

He looked sideways at Samantha. She didn't look like a Pennie Jarnigan but you never knew for sure until it was too late. Fidgeting with the buttons on his shirt cuffs, he tried to work up the nerve to ask his question.

All too soon they reached the drive up to the Bon Air Motel. Samantha stopped. It was steep and she knew she would be breathless by the time she reached the top.

"You don't have to come up. It's quite a climb."

"Hey, come on. I'm a good ole' mountain boy, remember. This is just a tiny ant hill to me. Unless you don't want me to come up. If you'd rather..."

"No, that's fine. I just..."

He took her hand and started to pull her up the drive. The chilled softness of her unringed hand felt good in his. He glanced at the flush on her cheeks as they climbed to the top and wondered if it was because of the steep hillside or because his hand was gently squeezing hers.

Standing on the stone balcony near Samantha's room, their view of the town was mostly blocked by the backsides of the storefronts below. Looking down the Parkway, though, the lights they had hardly noticed while in town glowed dimly through the dense early evening fog.

"What are your plans for tonight?" Conrad asked, his hand still holding hers. Hey, no squawk this time. His voice even sounded like he was in control of his hammering heart.

"We're taking the trolley around town to see the lights at 8:00."

"We?" Conrad felt disappointment lurch through his stomach. She wasn't alone. He prayed silently and quickly that she wasn't about to introduce him to some man she had come down here with. What kind of woman would play with him like that? He casually dropped her hand.

A small smile played on Samantha's mouth. "Yes, we. Kelsie's with me. We're going to see the lights. You know, on the trolley that goes around through town and up to the Arts and Crafts Community." Seconds passed before she worked up the nerve to add, "If you're not busy maybe you'd like to come along."

He purposely picked up her hand again before answering. "Yeah, I'd like that. Okay if I bring Lisa?"

It took a few tense seconds for her to remember who Lisa was. "Sure. Good idea. That'll give Kelsie something to do other than mope around us."

That wasn't so hard, Conrad thought, watching her lips move as she said spoke words that he barely heard. He wondered if they were as velvety as they looked and longed to check them against his own.

"Um...here's your jacket. Thanks a lot for letting me wear it. I forgot how cold it can get in these mountains when the sun goes down."

"You're welcome," he said as he slipped his arms into the still warm silky lining, breathing in the enticing mixture of his after-shave and her vanilla-sweet cologne.

"We'll meet you at the trolley stop, okay?"

"Sure, that'll be good. Well...I guess you better get inside before you catch your death," he said as he watched a shiver run through her body. "See you at quarter to eight then." As he turned to walk away he felt younger than he had in years. Take that, you old Pennie Jarnigan.

The spring in his step faltered just a little when he reached the downhill driveway. He thought of what he had waiting at home. Please God, don't let this one run away. He suddenly realized that the other women he had dated were only dress rehearsals for this one. Perhaps, with a lick of luck, this would be the beginning of the beautiful relationship he had always hoped to find.

Chapter 4

Samantha leaned against the door until long after he was out of sight. She resisted the urge to pirouette like a ballerina. How long had it been since she'd felt anything like this? Her mind paged back to when she first met David. Had she felt this excited then? She must have. Right? But tonight someone new and thrilling was prying his way into her heart, insistent and persistent. Someone..."Dang it! I don't even know his name," she said aloud.

Reaching her hand up to her mouth, she tried to physically remove the smile. No matter how many times she pulled the corners down, they popped back up again. Finally, she gave up. Kelsie was just going to have to wonder what was going on in Mom's head, as she did three quarters of the time anyway.

Conrad sat in his driveway watching the house. Inside was his new life, the one forced on him so painfully not quite a year ago. Justin was five now and Jessie three. They were his grandchildren and he had lived this past year almost solely for them. But tonight he would have given almost anything for a hot, hour-long, neck-deep soak in the old clawfoot tub upstairs. Thoughts of the woman he'd just met permeated his mind and he would have savored the chance to dwell on her in peace and quiet as the hot water swirled around his cold achy joints and muscles. He wondered how she would take the news of these children but wouldn't tell her tonight. No, tonight he would enjoy her company and let tomorrow take care of itself.

He forced his thoughts away from her and towards what he had waiting in the house. Slowly he opened the door of the van and stepped out. His pace picked up as he reached the porch and by the time he opened the front door he was ready and anxious to meet the needs of the family inside.

The kitchen door flew open amidst cries of "Grampy, Grampy. You're home. What'd you bring us?" The children bursting into the room flung themselves at Conrad. He swooped them up into his arms, kissing each of them in turn. Ada Pillars, his housekeeper, nanny and life-long friend, stood near the door patiently waiting to be heard over the racket.

"It's getting so a body can't get a word in edgewise with those two around," Ada said when the children stopped talking long enough to paw through Conrad's coat pockets. "Beef stew tonight. It's on the stove. Those two scalawags had a good day. Muffin got out so they chased her around the yard. Kept them out of my hair for a bit." She leaned down and petted the cat circling her ankles. "Good girl."

Conrad smiled. This woman had been there for him when he was a chubby, lonely adolescent; when his mom was gradually, painfully drinking herself into an early grave. He remembered waiting for her to pass out, then quietly locking the door and running down the sandy dirt road to Mrs. Pillars' house. Often as not she would be waiting for him in the porch swing and they would sway back and forth while they talked about everything but the reason he was there. Her husband, Carl, would sit in the faded wooden rocker and whittle silently through the evening, never making anything, never saying much, but companionable just the same.

Before he knew it, her voice would lull him to sleep. The next morning when he woke up in her spare bed, he would smell coffee perking and bacon frying. Hearing Carl's low deep voice discussing his plans for the day, he often wished they were his folks. Some days it was so strong that he almost prayed something would happen so he could stay forever under these quilts and in the security of this house.

She had always fed him well on these mornings, knowing that he never got enough healthy food at home. Eggs, bacon, fried potatoes, juice, fruit, and on some cold winter mornings even the dreaded mush. She told him years later that she had blamed herself for his weight problem, said she had taught him that food would sooth a troubled heart.

Now she was there to nurture and care for these kids. He couldn't say when she became Ada instead of Mrs. Pillars but it had brought a new dimension to their friendship. Many days she stayed with the kids so he could get some painting done or run errands. They had all needed her so desperately this past year, emotionally as well as physically.

"Okay, kids. Go get washed up. If you eat a good supper we'll read that new *Little Bear* book. Now scoot," Conrad said as he swatted both behinds toward the bathroom.

"Would you be able to come back tonight?" he casually asked as he walked Ada to the front door. "Around 7:30? I'm meeting someone in town to take the trolley tour and I'd like to bring Lisa with me. I know you spend plenty of time with these two but they'd be ready for bed and..."

"Now you hush. Of course I'll come back. That 'someone' wouldn't happen to be a lady, would it?"

"Yes, you snoopy ole' woman. A very pretty little lady, as a matter of fact." He ushered her to the door before she could ask any more questions. "You sure Carl won't mind? I hate to take you away from him in the evening."

"That husband of mine doesn't even know I'm in the house once he turns on that danged ESPN. All I do is sit and crochet, and I can do that here. I'll bring my overnight bag and plan on staying over. Then you won't have to worry about what time you get in."

She looked at him slyly then laid a hand across his bearded cheek. "I pray every night for you to find a nice girl. One that can make you happy." God knows you made a lousy choice with Julia, she wanted to add.

"At forty-six, I'm a little old to be looking for a nice 'girl', don't you think? Could get me in a heap of trouble if I was."

"You know what I mean, young man. Anyway, I'll see you in a bit."

"Tell Carl I said thanks," he hollered out the door as she climbed into her ancient Chevy. With a wave of her hand she was gone.

Supper in their house lately was either very amusing or a real trial. The kids' whole day came out through their actions and words. Tonight Justin wriggled incessantly through the supper blessing. Conrad had barely finished saying "Amen" when Justin erupted.

"Grampy, you shoulda seen Muffin today. She sneaked out when we went to get the mail."

"And..." Jessie tried to interrupt.

"Did you hang on to Jessie's hand when you got to the road like I told you?" Conrad asked.

"Course. Anyway, I went out and tried to get Muffin back in the house."

"And..."

"Jessie, let me tell it," Justin cried. "You'll just muss it up."

"Okay, but..."

"Anyway, Jessie ran behind Muffin and chased her right at me. But instead of coming to me she ran straight for the barn. You must not have shut the door tight this morning, Grampy, 'cause she squeezed right inside."

"Justin Lee, what have I told you about going in that barn when I'm not around?"

"I tried to tell him, Grampy, but..."

"Anyway," Justin scowled harshly across the table at Jessie "I pushed and pushed hard as I could on that door, and I think I must be getting a lot stronger 'cause it opened far enough to let me in."

"And I went and told Mrs. Pillars." Jessie said, arms crossed and head bobbing in triumph at finally being able to finish a sentence.

"So she came out and helped us chase Muffin outta the barn."

Conrad formed a mental picture of the three of them running helter skelter around the barn, Ada at half pace flapping that pink checkered apron of hers and the two kids screaming at the tops of their lungs.

How his life had changed from the days when he sat alone at this table quietly eating his supper, engrossed by the latest Dean Koontz novel.

"But..."

"Dog gone it Jessie. Will ya let me finish?"

"Better let him finish, sweetheart, or we'll all be eating cold stew. Cut it short now, buddy, or you won't have time for that apple pie over there on the counter."

"Pie! Oh boy! Is that for us? Mrs. Pillars said it was for somebody real special. Are you sure it's okay for us to eat it?"

"Silly boy," Conrad said. "Who do you think she was talking about? We're special, aren't we?"

"Holy cow, you're right," Justin said shoving a whole spoonful of stew into his mouth. "Come on, Jessie. Shut up and eat."

Lisa had been watching Conrad throughout the meal. He seemed to be only half listening to most of Justin's chatter, like he was on another planet or something. It wasn't until they were finishing up their pie that he gave her a clue of what was on his mind.

"Lisa, how would you like to go see the lights with me tonight?"

"Oh Dad, I was hoping I could take the car. A bunch of kids are going to the movie up in Sevierville and they wanted to know if I could be one of the drivers."

Conrad laid his fork down. "I don't ask much of you. Just this once can you do what I want instead of what you want?" His voice was harsher than he meant it to be. He forced himself to take a deep breath then added casually, "I met a woman in town today and we're going to see the lights. She has a sixteen-year-old daughter and I thought you could show her around."

Take her off your hands is more like it. Lisa was smart enough to keep this thought to herself. Looking across the table at her dad's face, she couldn't help but see how important this was to him. He tried to keep himself still but almost wriggled in his excitement, much as Justin had earlier. She had never seen him this nervous and it made her smile.

"Sure, Dad. No problem."

"Can we go too, Grampy? Please?" Justin was down from his chair and standing beside Conrad.

"Please?" Jessie stood on the other side, giving Conrad their infamous "one-two" punch. Though it usually worked quite well, this time he held firm.

"Not tonight."

"But we wanna..."

"I said no now. And I meant it. But if you're real good tonight and go right to sleep, maybe tomorrow we can go somewhere fun. I finished my painting today so I can take a day or two off. Okay?"

"Okay." Justin's face was hang-dog and Jessie forced hers into the same expression, even though the thought of getting to spend the day with her Grampy made her want to sing instead of pout.

As the kids ran for blankets, pajamas and their book Conrad checked his watch. He barely had time for their story and a quick shower but this ritual was something he wouldn't skimp on. It had become part of their evening routine and they needed his undivided attention.

This night, of all nights, Justin couldn't find his pajamas. After wasting five minutes looking for them, Conrad said, "I got it. Let's pretend it's a special night. Here, put on your new sweatsuit and pretend it's pajamas."

Justin grabbed the outfit from Conrad's hand and immediately stripped off his clothes.

"Grampy," Jessie whined. "Me too." She raised her arms, waiting for Conrad to help her take off her nightgown.

"Silly of me to think you wouldn't have to wear yours too, huh?" Conrad dug Jessie's hot pink sweats out of her drawer and helped her put them on.

He was real close to total exasperation by the time they finally snuggled down on the couch. With a child cupped in each arm, he began to read about Little Bear's new coat, shoes, hat and mittens. They fought, as usual, over who would get to turn the pages and tonight Conrad let Jessie win. Justin fumed for a while then sat quietly and listened. If the kids noticed he was reading a little faster than usual, they were too smart to say so.

Chapter 5

Samantha was anxious. It was 7:55. Maybe he wouldn't show? Maybe he had changed his mind? Maybe he was only pretending and didn't share the excitement she was feeling? Maybe...

"We didn't miss it, did we?" Conrad was beside her puffing a little from running that last block and dragging a protesting Lisa. The girls introduced themselves as the trolley pulled up then raced to a seat way in the back. From there they could watch both shows; their parents and the lights.

"Hey, Conrad, I didn't think I'd ever see you on one of these trips," the female guide said as they climbed up the steps.
"Hey, Kathy. How's it going?"

"Fine, but I'da thought you'd seen enough of these lights to last you for a while. Weren't you on the crew that had trouble getting all them strands to stay lit? Took you most of two extra days, didn't it?"

She looked inquiringly at Samantha, but Conrad just said, "We gotta get outta the way. I'll see you later."

When they had chosen seats on the right side, Conrad leaned in towards Samantha and said, "I was about halfway home before I realized I don't even know your name. I played a guessing game the rest of the way and on the drive back into town. Leslie, Carolyn, Becky, Susie...stop me if I'm getting close."

"Samantha. Samantha Jean Evers."

"Samantha, I never guessed that one, but it's perfect." He looked out the window and away into the night. "Perfect." He whispered it again so softly she almost didn't hear.

"And..."

"And what?"

"Well, I heard that girl call you Conrad, but is there more to it?"

"Conrad Ezekiel Richmond, at your service," he answered with a cavalier
mock bow.

"Ezekiel?" Samantha smiled as his middle name tickled her tongue.

"Actually it's Conrad Allen, but that seems blah, don't you think?"

Samantha laughed aloud and the sound reached the perked up ears of the two girls in the back seat. She turned to them and was met by a broad smile from Lisa and a stone-cold glare from Kelsie.

"What?" she mouthed before she gave up on reading Kelsie's mind and smiled up at Conrad instead.

He watched her while her attention was on the girls, waiting for her to turn back to him, knowing that he would do anything in his power to keep her this happy all night long. He'd gladly stand on his head and recite the latest redneck routine if that's what it took.

The passengers all settled in to enjoy the ride. The fog hadn't lifted and each light burned in its own small sphere. Three million lights in three million tiny, separate specks of brilliance. Their beauty was eerie through the dense fog.

Conrad enjoyed watching the lights reflect on Samantha's face and her child-like expressions. He sat close with his arm around the back of the seat, leaning into her each time a new set of lights were displayed, pretending he couldn't quite see from his side of the bench. His interest wasn't so much in the lights as in the feel of her hair gently catching in his beard as it brushed his cheek. The soft scent of her cologne, muskier and more sensual than the light vanilla fragrance that had entranced him this afternoon, nearly drove him insane. No, he told himself, this woman may be enjoying the lights like a child but she was anything but.

Samantha enjoyed the excuse for closeness and she let the scent of Canoe pull her into his side. She couldn't allow herself the pleasure of turning away from the lights and resting her lips against his neck. Not with Kelsie glaring at her. But, good Lord, she wanted to. She compromised by resting her head lightly against his shoulder, still watching the lights. When she did, Conrad pulled her tighter against him and laid his lips then his chin on the top of her head.

After a while they hardly heard the giggles or the coughs coming from the rear seat.

Samantha leaned up and whispered in Conrad's ear, "If all these three million lights went out at the same time, would that mean we'd be de-lighted?"

Conrad drew back a little so he could see the smile he knew would be on playing on Samantha's face. "Very punny, Samantha. But, yes, at least one of us would be very delighted."

Wow! A man who appreciates my humor, Samantha said to herself. She snuggled a little deeper into his side, comfortable to be sitting on the wooden bench beside him.

The lights were everything they had hoped for. Magical almost. As they headed out Highway 321, Kathy told them the history of the town. Sometimes she got so carried away with her stories that she forgot to point out the meaning of the lights that they had all come to see. She told of the much maligned Mr. Gatlin and how the town had named itself after him in order to get him to leave. She gave an explanation for each of the "bear" scenes, telling of how the bear was sort of a mascot for the town. Lit up versions of moonshine, quilting and crafting bears as well as many others lined the streets.

When they got back into town they enjoyed the tunnel of lights and the news that a good many marriages took place right there under those arches. The ritzy hotels vied for the award for "Best Light Display", and again it looked like River Terrace would win. Its multicolored lights on the framework of a train engine nearly took up the entrance to the hotel. The lights across the Parkway glowed with snowflake designs strung magically together with only beads of lights showing in the darkness.

"This set right here was the one Kathy was talking about." Conrad pointed at the arched light display beside the road. "Couldn't get them to stay lit to save our souls. What a pain." He seemed to enjoy telling Samantha little bits that Kathy was leaving out, mostly intentionally. What he enjoyed most was leaning into her hair and whispering in her ear.

They were acting like children who had never seen Christmas; laughing, giggling, pointing. The hour ride was over too soon and Samantha was momentarily appalled to think how little attention she had paid to the tour. She had been looking forward to it for months but she knew that she had missed nothing in comparison to what she had gained.

As they got off the trolley Kelsie grabbed Samantha's arm and pulled her aside.

"For crying out loud, Mom, act your age," she said, embarrassment and anger mixing in her voice. Samantha replied by sticking out her tongue. Kelsie turned on her heel and stalked away. Lisa caught up and tried to joke with her to lighten the mood.

"Come on. Let's go walk down by the river." Conrad tugged on Samantha's arm, hoping to erase the look of dismay on her face.

The multicolored lights on the train engine in front of the River Terrace Hotel looked even more impressive close up. As Samantha walked around the wire structure, her foot caught in a loop of cord and in an instant the whole scene went dark.

"Conrad?" Panic filled her high voice.

"There. Good as new," he said, straightening up from replacing the single plug into the socket. The girls were embarrassed by Samantha's clumsiness and raced away hoping to find someone more exciting to be with.

"Don't be out too late, Kelsie!" Samantha yelled after them.

"You either, Dad!" Lisa yelled back as she broke into fits of laughter.

"Kids," Conrad exhaled.

"Well, at least they've left us alone for a while."

Samantha wandered over to the iron bridge near the river and Conrad followed. While she looked down into the rocky, roaring river below he waited patiently. His arm grazed hers as she leaned forward with her hands pressing against the railing. He followed her gaze into the swirling water. She seemed to be staring at something but he couldn't for the life of him make out what.

She was immersed in thought about how fast things were moving, and she didn't mean the water racing below her. Beside her stood a handsome man who seemed perfect; friendly, caring, funny, with subtle and not so subtle passion lurking behind those dark brown eyes. Yet experience had taught her that if something seemed too good to be true, it usually was. But he seemed to be totally authentic. She chanced a glance at him and found him watching her. Caught in mid-thought, she stared back without expression.

They stood under the archway of lights, neither one noticing the people passing by. Unable to take the tension any longer, Conrad looped his arm around her waist and pulled her away from the coldness of the metal and into the warm length of him. His lips pressed inquiringly to hers, asking silently for permission to continue.

Everything was erased from Samantha's mind but answering with all the feelings that had been building inside her since she had first laid eyes on him six short hours ago. For a time they were unaware of anything but each other's warmth.

When they eventually separated they heard a smattering of applause. Looking around, they saw a small crowd had gathered.

"Let's go get a hot chocolate," Samantha whispered, her face looking like she'd spent five hours on a Lake Michigan beach without even a dab of sunscreen.

"Or maybe an ice cold shower," Conrad replied under his breath. When he grabbed her hand and started to pull her through the archway, she held back a little, still overwhelmed by the fire in his kiss.

They crossed the Parkway and wandered into a shopping area called The Village. Here the shops had an almost Colonial atmosphere. Conrad led Samantha through the crowd to the end of a line at a small place called The Jelly Jar.

"Best hot chocolate in town," Conrad explained, "or maybe it only seems that way because of Jim. He makes it special. You'll see."

When their turn came, the gray-haired man looked at Samantha appraising her from top to bottom.

"Conrad, good of you to bring a lady friend in for me," he said with a huge smile that went from one dimple to another.

"Sorry, Jim. I've got dibs on this one." He smiled into Samantha's eyes.

Jim took her hand after he sat two hot chocolates on the counter. Leaning forward he stage whispered, "Listen, why don't you ditch this guy and you and me'll go paint the town."

Samantha laughed a little nervously. "Sorry but I think I'll hang on to this one for a spell. Thanks anyway."

"I need this bottle of Joe's Hell Sauce too." Conrad playfully slammed the bottle down, just missing Jim's hand. Gently prying at Jim's fingers, he placed his money in the open palm.

"I'd say a dose of this might help," Jim said, ringing up their order. "Little lady, if you decide to get rid of this ole fuddy duddy, come on back," he hollered as they walked out the door. Through the window they could see him turn to the next couple in line and begin razzing them.

They let their hot chocolate cool then sipped on it as they wandered back to the main street. Samantha had to use two hands to steady the cup. Finally she drank her hot chocolate down almost greedily, preferring the warmth of Conrad's hand to the styrofoam cup. When it was gone, she threw the cup away and impulsively grabbed his empty hand. He smiled at her over the top of his cup, then pulled her arm through his while he drank the rest of his chocolate, leaving a slight milk line on his mustache.

Samantha wanted desperately to lick it off. Someday their relationship might be intimate enough to let her be comfortable with nibbling on his upper lip, but for now she used her napkin instead.

The action still seemed like a caress to Conrad and he puckered his lips as she wiped the milk away. Gently taking the napkin from her hand, he kissed her fingers, wishing all the while that he could pull them into his mouth. They were both aware of her breast resting against the back of his arm.

"How about a pizza?" Samantha said when the tingle in her fingertips started to invade the rest of her body. "I'm starved."

Conrad sucked air deep into his lungs. Damn, he muttered to himself as they headed to a crosswalk and stepped in front of a slow moving car. The driver hit the brakes hard then glared as they crossed in front of him.

Chapter 6

"When we came back from Nashville, I got a job at a factory up in Sevierville but I still hated assembly line work. So I quit four years ago. Abby was married by then and I had enough in the bank for Lisa and me to make it for a while even if none of my paintings sold. I owe a lot to Lucile. She's the one who convinced me that I had talent and insisted I set up in her shop and paint full time. It's worked out okay for both of us."

Samantha delicately bit a piece of pepperoni in two, trying not to end up with the whole piece in her mouth. She listened to him tell about himself, watching the corners of his eyes crinkle when he smiled. They sat in the booth furthest from the juke box. The Pizza Hut was packed tonight with tourists and the local kids who used it as a hangout.

"Hey, Mr. Richmond. Where's Lisa?" a teenage girl shouted from across the room.

"Hi, Gina. She's around town somewhere. I'm sure she'll end up here eventually."

"Cool. See ya."

"One nice thing about raising kids in a small town is that you know everyone. One bad thing about it is everyone knows you too and keeps a close eye on your every move. We'll be the talk of the town tomorrow."

"Sorry." But her teasing grin said she wasn't really. "Kelsie and I moved from a little burg to the "big" city when David and I divorced. My son, Jeff, got an apartment across town with some of his buddies. I thought that a big school would give Kelsie more choices. It did that, all right; more choices in drugs, alcohol, even guns. Scared the heck out of me the day she came home and told me she had to detour around two cop cars because there was supposed to be a gang war. And this wasn't even an inner city school. This was a nice, middle class, almost preppie school. I'll be glad when she graduates. At least there's still some hope left for the kids in my elementary school. Maybe things'll change."

Conrad watched Samantha, comparing her life in the big, scary city and his quiet one here. His train of thought derailed as he decided he liked the way her hair curled towards her face, liked the way she wiped the pizza sauce from her full lips, liked...

"Hey, Mom, buy us a pizza?" Kelsie stood beside their table with Lisa at her side. She seemed happy, but looked at Samantha with bitterness.

Conrad stood up and pulled a twenty dollar bill out of his wallet and handed it to Kelsie.

"My treat."

"I wasn't asking you," she snarled. "I was asking my Mom."

Lisa snatched the money out of Conrad's hand. "Never look a gift Dad in the mouth. Come on."

Samantha looked sternly at Kelsie's now glowering face. "Kelsie Marie, apologize. Now!"

"Sorry," but her harsh voice and steady glare said she was anything but.

"What should we get on our pizza?" Lisa grabbed her arm and dragged her away.

"Gina's over by the juke box," Conrad shouted to them. "You can sit with her if you want,"

"Trying to get rid of us, huh Dad?" Lisa shouted back, loud enough to be heard through the small restaurant.

Heads turned, strangers smiled knowingly, then went back to their own business. One man loudly said, "Ain't they the ones from the bridge?" Kelsie scowled back and forth between the man and her mother, wondering what had happened at the bridge. She gave Samantha one last dirty look and went over to the counter.

"What's got into her?" Samantha asked.

"Me, you, us."

"I suppose you're right." Her sigh came out deep and troubled. "I haven't given her much experience with sharing me. No one's ever interested me, so she's had me pretty much to herself."

"So now someone interests you?" Conrad stared at her until she could do nothing but look across the table and into his eyes. "Okay," she said after taking a deep breath. "Is this where I play games or do I simply give you an honest answer? I hate games, but seems like that's how it works. So, how much ammunition do I give you?"

"We don't need games, Samantha." His voice was deep, husky and reassuring.

"Then yes, I'm interested," she said before diverting her eyes to the pizza on her plate.

He reached for her other hand under the table. "Me too."

******

"Ready to go back to your motel or are you up to walking some more?" Conrad asked as they stood on the sidewalk outside the Pizza Hut. He caught Lisa's eye, pointed at his watch, and waved goodbye. Avoiding Kelsie's angry stare, he turned back to Samantha, definitely the warmer of the two Evers women. Being out of sight of this man was the last thing Samantha wanted. This evening could last forever and it would still end too soon.

"Will they be turning the lights out and rolling up the sidewalk soon?" she asked, hiding her uncertainty of what he meant about going back to her motel. Did he mean to be alone, or simply to end the evening?

"The lights stay on all night and they stopped rolling up the sidewalks for the Christmas season. We haven't walked towards the Park yet."

She took his hand in hers, relieved that, for the moment at least, no decision on how far she would let him go needed to be made. Walking easily, hand in hand, their hips swayed together in a gentle rhythm, comfortable now with each other's words and silences.

They ambled down to the other end of River Road, this one full of less expensive motels and less expensive lights but tonight someone could have put lights on an outhouse and they would have "oohed" and "ahhed" anyway.

Samantha talked about the Santas she made. Conrad listened with interest as she told him about the many personalities she discovered in their small sculpted faces. She told about her son, his wife and the baby they hoped would come before Christmas.

Conrad told of the many joys and only a few of the too many heartaches of growing up in these mountains. The only thing he neglected to mention was the kids. He had to tell her. Soon. But not tonight. Tonight was for magical belief in the happy-ever-afters of fairytales.

*****

Chapter 7

"I had a good time," Conrad said when their legs were ready to collapse and they gave up on the idea that they could make this night last forever. They stood in front of the stoop at her motel room door.

"Me too. It's been a long time since I've enjoyed myself this much. Lately my life's been pretty boring." Samantha held her wrist up under the porch light so she could see her watch. "Gee, midnight and I'm still awake. Will wonders never cease?"

"I'm sorry. I bet you're tired."

"Yeah, a little. Kelsie helped me drive but it was still a long trip."

"She seems like a good kid, even if she doesn't like me. You did a good job raising her."

"Yeah, thanks. Sometimes I wonder, you know."

"Me too. I remember when Lisa was fifteen. She about drove me nuts. Was Kelsie demanding and a total pain at that age?"

"Not as bad as my oldest and boldest, Jeff, but yeah pretty bad. I can't believe how overnight, I got really stupid. For fourteen years she believed every single word I told her, then all of a sudden I was the dumbest person in the world."

Conrad laughed loudly, remembering feeling the same way a couple of years ago. His laughter echoed off the surrounding cement walls.

"Shhh. You want to get me kicked out of here?"

He glanced over to the office where Bernie, the night desk attendant, sat in front the garish lights of the color TV.

"Bernie wouldn't do that. If he did, I'd have to tell Reverend Hulbert about how he was watching an old sleazy Madonna video when we walked past the office. The whole congregation would give him a lot of flack for that. Hey, Bernie, come on out here for a minute," he shouted loud enough for Bernie to look around, trying to figure out where the voice had come from and where he had heard it before.

Samantha grabbed Conrad's coatsleeve and pulled him into the shadow of the overhang. Surprising herself, she wrapped her arms around his neck and planted a firm kiss on his surprised halfway open lips. She latched on, effectively silencing him.

"I sure do like the way you shut a fella up," he said after a minute or two or twelve. His lips clung to hers, deepening the kiss. He tasted the combination of Dentine, Pizza Hut pepperoni and her own special flavor. For the moment all he could think of was following his tongue deep inside her. Pressing the length of his body against hers, he leaned in closer.

Samantha's back pushed against the ungiving cold wall as she responded. Lifting one leg slightly off the cement, she wrapped her foot around to meet the back of his leg. She shuddered as she relished the feel of him through their jeans. Her quick intake of breath almost pulled Conrad's tongue down her throat.

He groaned and simultaneously they broke apart. He was glad it was dark enough that she couldn't see the haze of passion clouding his eyes or the swelling in his jeans which she must have felt. Clearing his throat he said, "Where was I before I was so rudely interrupted?"

"Huh?" Samantha pushed her hair back out of her face although she actually wanted to pull it all forward and cover her cheeks. Her body had responded to his with a suddenness and ferocity she hadn't anticipated. Had he asked, she would have gladly laid down with him right then and there on the frigid cement. What a shameless hussy he must think she was.

Struggling to get control of her voice, she took his hand and pulled him back into the light. "You were getting ready to say goodnight, I'll bet."

"No, I don't think that was it. Oh yeah, I was going to ask you how long you are staying." Weeks, months, years. A lifetime of nights like tonight would be too short. Well, almost like tonight, he thought, a grin splitting his face.

"I have to be back to work Monday. We leave the day after tomorrow. This was just a quick trip to help us get through the coming winter."

"Well, I was wondering if you'd like to take a drive out to Cades Cove in the morning? I hear they've decorated for Christmas with old fashioned red bows, holly wreaths, that kind of thing."

Samantha looked into his eyes through her own hazy ones.

"I'd like that but what will we do with the girls?" Seconds passed before her mind cleared enough to let her add, "I mean, won't they be bored?"

Conrad grinned at the insinuation in her remark. Actually, he'd like nothing better than to be alone with her on a lonely nature walkway in the park. He thought longingly of the feel of her foot rubbing the back of his leg. Her tongue probing his mouth. Her... but, no, he wanted to introduce her to the kids. Time for them to get to know that part of each other would have to wait. He hoped desire would still be glazing her eyes when she found out about them.

"Lisa has her eye on a park ranger out in the Cove, some kid who was a few grades ahead of her in school. I'm sure they'd be entertained. I'll pick you up about 10:00, okay?"

"Uh huh. I mean sure. Ten o'clock." Her mind had unwittingly returned to the feel of his body against hers. She forced herself away from her depraved thoughts then added, "Maybe we better go in and wake the girls if we're going to get moving before noon."

"Soon," said Conrad stepping so close that his foot landed on her toes. He mouthed "Sorry" to her silent "Ouch" as he rested his lips tenderly on hers. He wanted to show her that passion wasn't the only feeling he had for her. After a mostly chaste minute he took the warm key from her hand, unlocked the door and let them into the room.

Kelsie lay dead to the world on the couch. Lisa stood up at the far side of the bed and yawned.

"'Bout time you got in. What'd I tell you about these late nights, young man? Do I have to ground you to get you to come in at a decent hour?"

"Come on, brat." Conrad grabbed her affectionately around the neck. "We gotta let these people get some sleep." He dragged her through the door. "See you at ten, Samantha."

Across the room Kelsie raised her head, her hair tousled from sleep.

"Night Sleeping Beauty," Conrad called out to her and wasn't sure in the flickering light of the TV if her hand flew up in farewell or an age-old obscene gesture of disaffection.

Samantha closed the door slowly behind Conrad and Lisa. She leaned her back against it, her fingertips running slowly across her lips, savoring thoughts of his lips on hers, trying to keep away thoughts of his jeans on hers. Hurrying through the room, she walked silently out on the balcony overlooking the driveway. Her eyes and heart followed the two shadows down the hill.

"Did you tell her, Dad?" she heard Lisa say.

"Shhhh," was the only sound Samantha heard drifting up the hill.

Chapter 8

Conrad leaned back in his overstuffed chair. The only light in the house was from the fire in the fireplace that he had lit to warm up. His mind drifted away...to a cold, rainy night not quite eleven months ago. Christmas Eve. His mind played games; it seemed like forever ago, yet it seemed like only yesterday. Abby had called early that morning to tell him that she and Jim were running up to Knoxville to pick up the set of Elvis TV trays that had finally come in for Jim's mom. Lisa had agreed to stay with the kids and they planned to be home in plenty of time for supper. Conrad, trying to finish framing and matting the painting he was giving them for Christmas, wiped off his hands and draped himself sideways across the ragged, well-worn chair that he kept up in his studio.

"Did the Santa suit fit?" Abby asked him.

"Luckily Santa has a little more padding than I do, but other than that it'll be fine."

They spoke for a while longer and arranged for him to come over at eight the next morning to surprise the kids.

"And, Dad, don't forget to cover that beard of yours real good or Justin will guess it's you."

"Yes, Abby," Conrad said, humoring her as usual. "Love you."

"Love you too. See you in the morning."

At 5:30 that night, Lisa called. Had he heard from Abby and Jim? No, but he assured her that they had probably been delayed and stopped for something to eat. They'd probably be home in a few minutes.

At 8:00, he called Lisa.

"Any word?"

"No. You?"

"Nothing."

"These two are getting pretty restless and bored. Think I should put them to bed?"

"Yeah, you can try. Abby can always wake them up to do stockings if she wants. I can't figure out what's keeping them."

He went to the window and watched the rain. It had started about an hour after they'd left. The temperature had dropped to 28 degrees shortly after that. He felt uneasy. Where were those kids?

At 9:21, a car pulled in the drive. The digital time on the VCR would be forever etched in his mind. He watched Sheriff Tate get out and walk toward the house. Conrad reluctantly met him on the porch. He remembered only vague patches of the conversation. Sorry. Yes, both of them. Slippery roads. Drunk driver. Didn't suffer. Help with the kids? Sorry.

John Tate drove him to Abby's house. The blue light from his cruiser flashed on the icy grass and Conrad asked him to please turn it off. Lisa had left the Christmas tree lights on and was curled up on the couch. He woke her and told her as gently as he could.

Lisa's tears burned like hot cinders on his chest as he held her tightly, swearing to never again let her out of his sight. Soon her tears mixed with his own. Their eyes turned to the bedroom door where the kids lay sound asleep.

Lisa tucked herself into a small ball on Conrad's lap, something she hadn't done since she was a tiny girl. Finally she dozed off. Conrad didn't think he would ever sleep again. Nothing would be the same. Nothing. Ever.

Justin woke up suddenly. "Christmas!" he whispered to himself. He sat up and rubbed the sleep out of his eyes.

"Jessie! Wake up, come on, wake up. It's Christmas!"

Jessie's eyes flashed open. Justin had reminded her about all the presents that would be waiting under the tree and she could hardly wait to see if Santa had brought her the puppy she'd begged and begged for.

"Santa came, Jess. I know he did. I saw his blue lights and everything. Did you know Santa had blue lights on his sleigh? Neither did I, but I saw them flickering all over the yard. I peeked out the window when I got up to go potty last night. He musta been on the roof 'cause I only saw the lights, not his sleigh or reindeer or nothin'."

"Did you see my puppy?" Jessie asked.

"Nope, but I'll bet he had him under his coat cause it was rainin'. Come on, let's go see what he brung us."

Hand in hand, they ran to the living room.

Conrad heard their footsteps too late to intercept them. The first thing they saw was the brightly lit tree with no presents. They turned in unison to the unmistakably empty stockings hanging over the fireplace.

"I didn't see him," Justin wailed. "Honest I didn't. I saw his lights but nothin else. Then I covered my head real good. Why didn't he leave us any presents, Grampy? Lisy, did you get presents?" He started to cry.

Jessie stood behind him, her eyes filled with disbelief. Following Justin's lead, as always, she began to cry too.

Conrad knelt in front of them, tears streaming down his face.

"Wait, Grampy, why isn't Mommy up? Where's Daddy? I'll go get 'em. Mommy will know what happened to Santa." Justin ran to his parents' room. "Mommy? Daddy?" Conrad picked Jessie up and followed him. Once inside, he closed the door and proceeded to horribly alter the lives of two innocent, unsuspecting children.

Chapter 9

While Conrad relived the most painful night of his life, Samantha lay curled up on her side of the double bed thinking about the evening.

"Did you have fun tonight, Kels?"

"Uh huh," came the groggy reply from the other side of the bed. "Don't have to ask if you did, do I?"

"What makes you say that?" She couldn't keep the grin out of her voice.

"Maybe the fact that you were climbing all over him." Kelsie rolled over, warming to the conversation, coming fully awake now. She propped herself up on her elbow before adding "It was almost disgusting."

Samantha sat up. "Disgusting?" How much had she seen? "Are you saying I was not behaving like a woman should with a man, or just not like your Mom should?"

"Well, it just seems like..."

"Like what? Like I should live my life only for you, through you? Never find my own happiness? Is that what you want? You have your friends and your life but I shouldn't have anyone."

"Mom, I never said that. It only seems like you are getting a little carried away with this guy. You only met him today and already you're about to jump his bones."

"Kelsie, where do you come off saying that?" Samantha wasn't about to admit how close she was to the truth. "And if anyone knows how I've hoped to find someone special, you do."

"Well, you don't even know him. Maybe, just maybe, he's not the angel you think he is."

Rolling over on her back, Samantha closed her eyes. "Goodnight," she said then pretended to be asleep so that Kelsie would leave her alone.

Single life certainly wasn't all it was cracked up to be. She remembered how she had kidded around with her friend, Clarise, that their only hope of finding a decent man was to sit on the courthouse steps and wait for one to finalize his divorce. Otherwise, once they left the courthouse grounds, they were snatched up like prize pork at the county fair. She smiled in the darkness at her unintended pun.

Insecurity had been part of the roller coaster ride. Was she too fat? Too old? Too gray? Too frumpy? Anything that could possibly be wrong was. On rare days when she could be honest with herself, she admitted that she looked better than she had in years. She'd lost weight and her hair looked healthier now that she'd stopped dying it. But the biggest difference was in her face. Looking at old pictures of herself she had seen the way her brow had puckered and her lips had seemed frozen in an unrelenting frown.

Nowadays, most of her problems were in her mind. The roller coaster ride of middle-aged hormones chased her from the heights of euphoria to the depths of depression in less than sixty minutes flat. For reasons known only to God, her moods would rise and fall like a hot air balloon on a gusty day.

So she took her mind off Mr. Right or the lack of him. Instead she planned and schemed for her future. The shop she hoped to open one day seemed right at her fingertips. In this fantasy, everything was good, bright and possible. She could envision her store, filled with country softness and happy people. Flowers and stone walkways in the yard seemed so close that she could smell the fragrant lilacs if she tried hard enough.

She could almost see the dust motes in the sunshine that streamed through the huge front window, the sign on which read "Samantha's 'Tiques and Tummies". Inside she would bake up the quick breads she had been saving recipes for and sell country antiques, many that she had scouted out and refinished herself. There would also be the primitives whose surfaces were too precious to be touched by anything but a soft dust rag.

Seconds, minutes, lifetimes later everything would vanish. Something more wicked than black magic made it all disappear. She watched the flowers wither as the vision grew fuzzy and finally faded into darkest night. What she prayed was not reality set in, sinking her in the quicksand traps of her mind. Depression filled her soul.

While all the ups and downs raged through her mind she had begun to date. But none had ever worked out. Some men had wanted a woman to depend on them, to smother them with affection and spend every waking moment with them. That wasn't for her.

Some seemed to have read too many recent issues of Cosmopolitan magazine. Hoping to use her mind as a route to her bed, one had asked all evening "How do you feel about that?" or "How did you react when that happened?" She wanted to scream at him that if he wanted to know her innermost thoughts he'd have to stand in line and when she figured them out, she'd let him know.

Then there was the question of sex. Some men wanted to get skin-to-skin close first. Then maybe, and only maybe, mind-to-mind close. Although she sometimes craved the caresses of a man, none of these men had the touch she longed to feel and she abstained from intimacy.

But Conrad was different. Oh, yes he was. She lay there, remembering how his fingers had held the brush to the canvas. Thoughts of him stroking her as delicately seeped furtively into her mind. Through the evening they had laughed and joked, but the serious moments had been even more wonderfully special. She felt comfortable with him, not worrying about every word she said. Every move she made seemed right.

She looked over at Kelsie's sleeping face. The anger had been erased for now, but she knew it would be back when they woke in the morning.

"You've got to understand, honey," she said, barely above a whisper. "This one rocks my world."

Kelsie moaned in her sleep, grabbed a handful of blanket and rolled away. Samantha settled down in what was left of the covers. The warm feeling surging through her body had nothing to do with the blanket covering her.

"My turn." Laying quietly in the bed, she thought she would finally fall off into a dream-filled, Conrad-filled sleep. But half an hour later she was still wide awake, twisting and turning; back to front, side to side, even up on her knees with her head buried under the pillow. Suddenly the flannel nightgown seemed too warm. It had coiled around her waist like a wild grapevine around a black walnut tree and she tugged at the hem.

"Geez, Mom," Kelsie complained as she grabbed her pillow and blanket and stumbled across the black room to the couch. "Now at least one of us can get some sleep. Chill out, will ya?"

"Sorry, Kels. I can't seem to get comfortable. Guess I ate too much pizza."

"Yeah, sure, like that's your problem."

Samantha smiled. "Yeah, like that's my problem," she whispered, unwilling and unable to share more of the feelings racing through her mind and her body.

Chapter 10

All Conrad wanted to do was think of Samantha snuggled into his chest, but memories of the past year kept creeping into his mind.

"Why the hell did you even bother to come home, Julia? All you've done since you got here is bitch and cry." Conrad could barely stand the sight of this woman who had controlled him and his daughters for so many years. She had returned one day before the funeral, and now, one day after, he could hardly wait until she left.

"How dare you say that to me? I buried my favorite daughter today."

"What? For God's sake, Julia, shut up! Do you want Lisa to hear you? We buried our oldest daughter and I better never hear you say otherwise. Understand?"

"When did you become so mean, Conrad? She was my baby and now she's gone."

"If she was so special, why'd you walk out on her? Do you know how hard she cried when you moved to California? Who was there for her then? Who was there to help her and Jim through that tough pregnancy with Justin? Who got the call the night Jessie stopped breathing? It sure wasn't you, was it? Hell no. You were too busy with that gigolo you so fondly called a boyfriend. By the way, where is golden boy?"

"He left me two months after I moved to California. I heard he died of AIDS last year."

"Did...did he infect you?" Conrad asked quietly.

"How sweet of you to care. No, he started seeing men after he left me. Besides, how do you know I didn't give it to him. Maybe it's even alive in you right now, waiting for just the right time to make your life as miserable as you've made mine."

"You always were a bitch, Julia. If you had given me AIDS, half of the men in these mountains would be dying too, wouldn't they? Heaven knows you slept with enough of them." He dared her to argue.

"You make me sick. You're always so 'Holier than thou', aren't you? Well, I don't need this crap. I'm going home."

Conrad lowered himself into the kitchen chair, trying to rub the exhaustion and pain out of his eyes. "I suppose I was being foolish to think you'd want to help with the kids."

"Lisa's a big girl now..."

"The little kids, Julia. Your grandchildren. Justin. Jessie. You know, the ones who lost both parents a four days ago."

"Don't you use that tone with me. I don't need it. If you think I'm going to come back here and be a mother hen to those sniveling babies you are out of your damned mind. I had a hard enough time taking care of my own two. Geez, Lisa was always so whiny and bratty."

"It's called asthma. She outgrew it before she was seven. She was miserable so how'd you expect her to act?"

"Well, she was never a sweet little girl like Abby."

"Dammit, Julia. Go upstairs, pack you bags and get the hell out of here. I guess I don't need your help and I hope you never come back."

"Me either, Mom." Lisa's meek voice came from the doorway where she leaned leadenly against the door jam.

Conrad glared at Julia before going over to stand in front of his daughter. Pulling her chin up, she had no choice but to look in his eyes.

"Honey, how long have you been standing there?" Her tears threatened to overflow and he knew she'd heard much more than any child should hear from their own mother. Not only had she lost her sister, now she had lost what was left of her love for her mother. He folded his arms around her shaking form as the tears spilled.

He turned his head toward Julia. "Get out! Get Sheriff Tate or somebody to give you a ride up to Knoxville. His number's by the phone." Without another word he helped Lisa to the sanctuary of her room.

Two o'clock came and went. Samantha pulled off the now soggy nightgown and threw all the covers but the sheet to the other side of the bed. If she thought this would help her sleep, she was lasciviously mistaken. The softness of the sheets caressed her nakedness and a different friction point rubbed across her body each time she moved. Sleep, she told herself. Do you want bags under those baby blues of yours?

Think of something else, she told herself sternly. Try as she might, nothing but Conrad came to mind. She lifted her head to look again to look at the clock on the bedside stand; 3:27. Climbing out of bed, she drew the damp, wrinkled nightgown over her head.

Quietly she opened the door to the balcony, slipped out and made sure the door was not locked behind her.

The mountains in back of the motel reflected what little light there was and she gazed at them as she stood with her arms braced against the cool wooden railing.

"Is this why you've brought me back here all these years?" she asked the moon. To meet this man. This wonderful, glorious, sexy, down to earth, funny...Whoa, hang on here a second, she told herself sternly. He's human, afterall. Don't try to make him out to be more than he is. But, oh, what he is.

She sat down in the chaise lounge and tucked her nightgown snugly around her legs. It was cool, especially in the damp gown. Too much of a bother to go back in for a blanket, she pulled her legs up to her chest and forced herself to ignore the chilly plastic that wrapped the chair.

This town had sang it's siren song to her for years. She had first seen it as a teenager, looking for and finding the hulking mountain boys. But it had been the mountains themselves that drew her back time and again. She had implanted her love of this place into Kelsie's spirit as well.

Now she had met a man who brought it all together. She wondered how she could fall so hard, so fast, so completely. Always the practical one, she weighed all the possibilities, almost to the point of missing out on the chance to enjoy the results. She never lost control of her emotions, never let herself go, hated roller coasters because of it. But here she was, putty. Silly putty at that, ready to take whatever shape he wanted. With Conrad it would always be bright and beautiful, just like the lights that still glowed from the lampposts below her.

Wouldn't it? Doubt reached its loathsome fangs into her mind, trying, as always, to suck the blood out of her happiness. "Nothing and no one is ever perfect!" it screeched at her. Something would go wrong. Something always did. Always.

"No," she said aloud. "Not this time. I'm not going to spoil it this time. Go away," she told the dreaded darkness and it receded, for now, to the back of her mind.

Two days after the still-rankling scene with Julia, Conrad had stopped at Jim's parents' house. They'd argued long and hard with him but he held firm and insisted there be only one funeral. They wanted their boy all to themselves and resented his interference on behalf of the children. The only compromise he could stomach was to let them have time alone with Jim's casket after Abby was lowered into the ground.

He felt their hostile eyes on him through the gap in the curtains as he walked up on the rotting porch. They let him pound on the door for a good five minutes before they accepted the fact that he wasn't going to leave before having his say.

"Alright, what do you want, Richmond?" The man who finally came to the door was dressed in a holey V-neck T-shirt and wear-shiny dark green work pants. Tobacco stained the front of the shirt and Conrad didn't want to think about what stained the pants.

"I need to talk to you about our grandchildren, Hank. Martha, it's cold out here. Mind if I come in?"

Martha sat on the couch in the shadowy living room, a rip in the front of her robe showing a yellowed slip or gown beneath. Her mousy gray hair was dull and disheveled. "Please let him come in for a minute, Hank. Please."

Hank stood aside, muttering under his breath as Conrad walked past him and into the house.

Once inside, Conrad could think of little else than getting out. The room reeked of unwashed bodies and stale cooked cabbage. Martha's face was sallow against the once brilliant yellows and oranges of the couch. Hank sat on the footstool at her feet, making sure Conrad felt as unwelcome as possible.

"Make it fast. You know you ain't welcome here. Say your piece'n go."

"Fair enough. Jim's kids need you. They need all the love they can get right now. I'd like you to help me raise them. With my painting and all, I can't do it alone. Even with Ada helping, it's too much."

"Maybe if you'd get yourself a real job, instead of wasting all that time on artsy fartsy stuff, you'd make enough to support you and them kids." Hank's face was sarcastic, somehow thinking that he'd bested Conrad.

"I'll make more money off one painting of an old garbage can than you'll make from a whole year of disability checks, old man." Conrad took a deep breath, knowing his display of anger had probably blown any hopes he might have had with them. "Sorry. It's been a bad time for all of us. I...I was wondering if you could take them a couple of days a week." He hated apologizing and hated asking anything of these people. The thought of those two kids here in this house turned his stomach. But he needed help and the kids needed more love than he could give them so he quietly waited for their reply.

"You've got more nerve than brains, you damnable fool. Jim was our only child, all we had in this world. He's dead and now you think we've got some feelings for his kids. Well, you're wrong. We never have wanted anything to do with you or yours. I made that clear from day one, didn't I?"

"But these kids are a part of Jim. They're all you have left. Martha, can you honestly tell me you don't care what happens to them?"

"Yep," Hank spat out, answering for his wife who seemed to be fading into the flowers of the couch. A small stream of spittle mixed with tobacco juice dripped down his stubbled chin. "Now get the hell out of my house. And never let me see you on my land again or you'll find yourself looking down the wrong end of my shotgun. You got that?"

Conrad stood up. Jim had been a good man but the less his kids knew about these people the better off they'd be. He stalked out without speaking.

Opening the van door, he turned to find Martha scurrying up to his side. Holding her robe closed with one hand, she rested the other on his arm. Her nails looked gray against her pink skin and Conrad had to force his arm to stay steady and not pull away in revulsion. She looked anxiously over her shoulder at her husband's figure in the doorway.

"Jessie is eatin' again, ain't she? I heard she stopped eatin' since...well, you know. Hank don't mean no harm, Conrad. He's just a lost soul. We both are. I don't know what'll become of us." She started to cry and turned back to the house.

Conrad softened at the sight of the abused woman shivering in her housecoat. "I'll take good care of Jim's children, Martha. And I'll be around if you need anything," he shouted as the door slammed behind her.

Samantha went back inside the motel room and crawled into bed, pulling all of the covers back over her, head included. I've got to get some sleep, she complained silently. Pure exhaustion overtook her and she was out like a light when the alarm went off at 8:30.

Conrad buttoned the red and black checkered flannel shirt over his t-shirt. He stared at his reflection in the mirror, still unable to stop the memories from overtaking his mind.

The healing process slowly but surely began. He spent every waking minute with the kids and was seldom out of their sight. Jessie started to eat, her body's needs finally conquering her heart-rending sadness. Justin occasionally would mutter a few words when Conrad spoke directly to him. Some days it was two steps back for each step forward but there came days when every so often smiles would be passed between them.

Never one to date much, Conrad felt a sudden need of female companionship. He wanted someone not only for the emotional and sexual release but also someone to talk to about raising kids. Someone to help him figure out what he was doing wrong and to cuddle with on long, quiet evenings. Besides, after the kids went down for the night and Lisa had gone out or to her room it got mighty lonely.

So he began spending his Saturday evenings at a local dancehall. Watching the line dancers, he was unable to figure out how they knew when to turn or where to step next. How they missed tripping over their own two feet was beyond him. What ever happened to the box step his mother had made him stumble over when he was a kid? At least that dance brought you in close contact with the female of your choice.

At a bar up in Knoxville one night a pretty little red head sat down beside him, breathless from twirling around the dance floor. Small talk led to intimate talk and they ended up at her place. The release felt good, even in the condom, and her body was warm, soft and willing. But as soon as they were satiated, she got up and fixed herself a stiff drink, offering the glass to Conrad after she had guzzled half of the contents. He took a small sip and handed the glass back to her, watching her carelessly empty the glass and pour another. Intentionally he brought up the children and started whining about how hard his life was. He told her how he sure could use a woman around to help out. Before long she was ushering him out the door, telling him how great he was and that she would be sure to call him one day real soon. Conrad wiped the sweat off his forehead and smiled at his gentle escape as he walked to his truck.

"Lessons learned, Conrad ole' boy," he mumbled to himself.

After that he was more cautious about who he dated. A lady from the phone company had been congenial, circumspect and wouldn't sleep with him on the first date. He convinced himself that was a plus. After they had been going out for a while, he invited her home for supper. All went well for the first hour. Jessie watched her shyly and Justin acted like a charming prince. Supper, however, brought out the worst in both of them. She left in a huff when Justin flipped overcooked peas out of his spoon, which happened to land in green blobs on her new silk dress.

Turning on him she said, "You told me you had kids, not Dr. Jeckle and Mr. Hyde. Call me when they go away to college."

"What do you want some dumb lady for when you got us?" Justin asked before she had her car turned around in the driveway.

Conrad listened to her car spitting gravel half way to the road then gave Justin an exasperated glare. "There's things you don't understand."

Justin and Jessie stared at him innocently for a long moment. They looked at each other, then back at him.

"Well? We're waiting. You always say if you don't know something ask. So I'm askin'. What can some puny old gal give you that Jessie and I can't? We can smootch you a lot and we won't slobber on ya like we saw her doin'. And we hug and squeeze you already. So why would you want some dumb weird lady around?"

"Never mind, you goofy boy. Come back when you're sixteen and not a day before." Conrad grabbed Justin out of his chair and started to tickle him. Soon the kids had forgotten all about the conversation and Conrad had buried his need for a woman once again.

Forcing his mind back to the present, Conrad pushed up his sleeve to check his watch. If he didn't hurry he'd be late and that sure wasn't the way he wanted this day to start.

He was scared. Scared beyond all logical thought that Samantha would turn tail and run like the others. And who would blame her. Women her age certainly weren't looking for a bunch of kids to raise.

"Please let her be different," he said towards the ceiling as he hurried out of the bedroom. "Please."

Chapter 11

On the trip into town Conrad brought up the subject of the woman and teenager they were about to meet.

"Do you guys remember when that lady came out for supper with us a few months ago."

"The one I flicked peas at?"

"Yeah, that's the one," Conrad answered through his teeth.

"Oh no! That's not who we're picking up is it? She hates me. I didn't mean to make a green mess on her new dress. Honest."

"No. Not her. This is a woman I met in Lucile's store yesterday when I was painting. Lisa met her last night. She's nice isn't she, Lisa?"

"Yeah, a real peach."

Conrad glanced over at her, trying to read a deeper meaning into her words.

"I like peaches," Jessie volunteered quietly.

"Thanks, Jess. Anyway, what I'm telling you...no, what I want to ask you is to be nice to this lady because she's really special. It's important to me that we all make a good impression. Okay?"

"Sure," Justin agreed too easily. "But can I get peas for lunch?"

Conrad slammed on the brakes as traffic light #5 turned red in front of him. He spun around and glared harshly at Justin.

"Geez, Grampy. I meant that I'm really hungry for peas is all. Can't a kid be hungry for peas?"

When they got to the Bon Aire, Lisa hurried ahead and knocked. When Kelsie opened the door she grabbed her arm and said "Come on. Let's get out of here quick." She flashed Conrad a thumbs-up sign as they ran past.

Samantha threw her purse strap over her shoulder and almost had the door closed behind her before Conrad gently took her arm.

"Wait a second. There's something I need to tell you. Let's go back inside. It'll only take a minute."

Samantha watched the anxious look in his eyes as she walked backwards into the room.

"I knew it. You're an axe murderer. Well, we can overcome that. With a little love and ..." She stopped suddenly, realizing that Conrad wasn't in the mood for jokes. "What?" she whispered, holding the breath that caught in her throat.

He sat down on the bed and motioned for her to sit beside him. "I wasn't completely honest with you last night," he said quietly after inhaling a deep breath.

Told you so, told you so, a bitter little voice sang from the back of Samantha's mind. There's always a down side, the voice chided. You ignored me last night, didn't you? You really expected otherwise? You should have known. How could you think this guy would be any different? Fool!

Conrad waited for her attention to return to him before telling her about the two children in the van, how they'd got there and how they had changed his life. He watched her eyes for signs of rejection and found it, plain and simple. He sensed her pulling away with each sentence he spoke, though her body never moved. By the time he finished his story he knew he had lost her and nothing he could say would bring her back.

"I'm sorry I didn't tell you first thing last night. I needed time to let you get to know me before I sprang them on you. I know, that wasn't being entirely honest but I didn't know 'til it was too late that things would heat up as quickly as they did." He forced a smile at the unintentional pun but she only stared at him. "Does it have to make such a difference, Samantha?"

She stood up and crossed the room to the window, for once not seeing the mountains in the distance.

"Dammit, dammit, dammit," she muttered under her breath. Suddenly she turned on him. "For God's sake, Conrad. Make a difference? How could it not make a difference? I've raised my kids. I've loved them, kissed away their tears, and tried to fight their battles for over twenty years. It's my turn. I've got plans of my own and I spent last night trying to figure out how to make you part of them. I was hoping...Oh hell, what does it matter now?" Angry at herself, Conrad and the rest of the world, she paced the room, muttering under her breath.

Conrad was surprised. He'd expected her to have reservations, had almost convinced himself that he could overcome them. But he was unprepared for this embittered outburst. Where was the woman he fell in love with last night? Fell in love with? Oh Lord, is that what I've done? Yes, he forced himself to admit before going on with his thoughts. How could he have misjudged her so badly?

Listening to her rant, he felt anger building; from his mind, to his gut, to his heart.

"You think I liked the idea of raising Abby's kids? You think I wanted to be saddled for another fifteen years? I raised Abby and Lisa by myself when their mother left." He yanked his wallet from his jeans pocket and pulled out a well-worn piece of paper. "See this? Do you know what this is?"

Samantha refused to look at what Conrad waved in her face.

"It's a plane ticket. To Jamaica," he continued anyway. "It was to be Abby's Christmas present to me. I found it in her top dresser drawer when I was going through her things. It was her way of saying that I'd earned my turn. By the time I found this it was too late, not that it would have made a dammed bit of difference. Those kids are mine now, lock, stock and barrel, and I love them more than anything in this world." Sadness cloaked his eyes as he slowly turned away from her. "Including whatever I'd hoped you and I would have," he said more to himself than to her.

What now? No answer jumped out at him and he sat with his chin against his chest; dejected, rejected and lonelier than he'd ever been in his life.

After a while Samantha came over and sat on the bed beside him. She had grumbled herself through the first shock. It was one of the hardest things she'd ever done to watch his heart ache.

"Conrad?"

No answer.

"Conrad, I...I wish I could say 'oh, how sweet, no problem' but I can't help how I feel."

Conrad fiercely pulled her close, surprising her as he pushed her down onto the bed. He buried his face in her hair then roughly kissed her lips. Part of him wanted to hurt her as much as she was hurting him. He rolled on top of her, mindlessly hoping to overpower her mind more than body. At first Samantha tried to push him away but his fire and the way she felt about him soon had her clinging to him, responding with every inch of her body to the rekindled passion that had begun smoldering the night before.

Conrad came to first. *What am I doing?* The door was unlocked and some very surprised kids could come in at any minute. He shoved himself away from her and lay on his back, his arm across his eyes as he tried to catch his breath as well as his sanity. For a while neither one spoke.

"Sorry," he said not moving his arm. Shame racked his senses. He had to explain, couldn't let her think he was a monster.

Samantha tried desperately to breath normally. Finally, when she could speak, she said "Conrad, please, it's nobody's fault. We just got carried away, that's all."

"Yeah, after I damned near..."

"Shhhh! Don't say that. I was every bit as willing as you," she admitted, running her fingers along the back of his thumb.

Conrad thought he would die when he saw the tears start to fall from her eyes. He already missed her glowing smile and the way it had lit up the night better than the three million lights they'd seen from the trolley.

"I'm sorry," he said again, summing up all of his feelings into two words.

"Me too. What really hurts," Samantha hiccuped, "is that I still care about you and I still want to be with you. But I can't. No, I can't let us be together."

Conrad pulled her into his arms, wishing there was some way...

"Well then, I guess I better get out of here," he said, letting her go minutes later. He was ready to bolt through the door when he had another thought. "Mind if we borrow Kelsie for the day? Lisa's pretty excited about having someone her own age along."

Kelsie would want to go, even if it meant dealing with Conrad. The two girls had already formed an affinity that had been missing in Kelsie's life. Samantha thought about the long, lonely day ahead. Sure, she could go out shopping in Pigeon Forge or drive up to Newfound Gap alone. Isn't that what she wanted. To be alone in these mountains? But she knew she'd spend the whole day thinking about him, wondering what he was doing at any and all given minutes and wishing she was there, enjoying his company and his smile.

"Listen, we had a nice day planned. It would be a shame to disappoint everybody. Can't we just pretend that nothing has changed? For their sake?"

Conrad stared at her. Was she maybe, just maybe, willing to give them a try, at least meet the kids before she decided to ditch him and them? If she was around them for a while she'd see that they were no trouble. Just a couple of sweet angelic kids was all.

"I'd like that," Conrad answered in a low, undeniably sexy voice. "But maybe you ought to fix your face. Your lipstick is smeared and that black stuff around your eyes makes you look like a raccoon. I do have a reputation around here for being a nice guy, and I'd hate like heck to blow it now." He tried to smile. She tried to smile back. Neither one could quite pull it off.

Samantha looked into the mirror over the bathroom sink as she removed the makeup she had so carefully applied an hour earlier, replacing only the lipstick. Raising her gaze to meet her eyes, she saw that the haunted look was back, the unhappy phantom of too many miserable years. Why had she let him in like that? She knew better than to let anyone get close to her.

"You are a hopeless idiot," she silently mouthed to her reflection.

Conrad waited for her by the door, opened it and let her pass through. Her shoulder brushed against his chest and he controlled the urge to grab her and drag her back into the dusky room.

"Don't get your hopes up, Conrad," she turned to say as she walked past him. "It's only for today then I'm gone. You hear?"

He followed her with his head down and his hands deep in his pockets. Damnable woman!

What was that brown gunk on Jessie's face and hands? As he got a closer look, he knew. Chocolate! And there it was encircling Justin's mouth too. Cocoa-colored splotches streaked the side windows, from small handprints into smeared globs. Conrad stalked to the van and yanked the door open. Lisa saw his face and shrank down in her seat, knowing full well that she would get the blame for this one.

"Grampy, Grampy, Grampy!" mixed with "Dad, I..." and "What took ya so long Grampy? We been waitin' here for hours. Let's go."

Conrad's anger evaporated as quickly as it had come. These were his kids come hell or high water. Either she liked them or she didn't. No more pretending they were perfect. This was how they were. Like it or lump it.

Samantha walked up and peered into the van. Every eye was trained on her, waiting for her reaction. She reached past the sticky doorway without looking at Conrad. Smiling, she took Jessie and Justin's gooey hands in hers without flinching.

"Come on you tootsie rolls, let's see how much of this mess comes off. I want to see if you're as cute as your Grampy said you are." She led them back to her room, explaining who she was and talking about the fun they were going to have.

Conrad stayed behind to clean the windows. Lisa and Kelsie slunk past him with wary grins.

"Whew!" Lisa whispered to Kelsie not quite out of earshot.

Kelsie looked back and muttered, "Men are so stupid!" barely loud enough for Conrad to hear.

Chapter 12

Conrad watched as Samantha almost clung to the door on her side of the car, as if she wasn't comfortable breathing the same air. She yawned incessantly as she watched the river that snaked along with the winding road.

"Sorry if I bore you," he said testily when he noticed her trying to stifle a huge yawn.

"What? Oh, I'm sorry. No, one thing you don't do is bore me." Her eyes met his for a moment as he tried to keep the van on the road that curved back and forth through the trees. "It's just that I didn't sleep too well last night. I guess I was too warm."

"Warm? It got down to thirty-five degrees. You call that warm?"

"I didn't say it was the temperature that made me warm, now did I?"

Conrad swerved the van back on the road after letting the last look at her grinning face rest a fraction of a second too long. What was that supposed to mean? Was it possible that she'd been thinking about him and the kisses they'd shared?

His jeans tightened. The sound of the car horn behind him brought him back to the present. Checking the speedometer, he noticed that it had fallen to twenty. He stepped hard on the gas and listened to the tires squawk beneath him.

"Hey, Dad?" Lisa said as she hung over the back of his seat, her face full in his rearview mirror. "You got a problem? Want me to drive?"

"Shut up, Lisa. I'll manage. And get your seat belt on." He glanced again at Samantha who was smirking, her pose more relaxed now. He wished he could stop worrying about the future that had seemed so bright in the glowing lights of downtown Gatlinburg last night. He twitched in the seat, trying to make up his mind that he could calm down too. So what if she wouldn't be here for all the tomorrows he had hoped for? So what if she wasn't the answer to his prayers? So what if she was tearing apart his mending heart? So what?

He jerked the van into a parking place in front of a sign that read "Quiet Walkway".

"I'm walking," he barked as he climbed out his door, adjusting the uncomfortable tightness in his jeans before anyone could notice. Except Samantha. She seemed to notice and understand every move he made. "Come or stay, it's up to you."

He stalked ahead on the trail, leaving the rest to follow if they wanted. At this moment he truly didn't care. He needed to walk off the frustration that was settling in his mind and in his groin.

Samantha decided it was best to give Conrad and the kids a little time to themselves. She sat beside the small stream, tossing pieces of sticks into the rushing water, watching them swirl away from the edges into the fast current near the middle. An otter swam out into the creek, playing with a rock. She turned, anxious for someone to share this unusual sight with her. But there was no one. Get used to it, she reminded herself.

Lisa and Kelsie trudged back up the path with Justin and Jessie.

"We couldn't keep up with Dad. He's probably half way to Cherokee by now." Lisa plopped down beside Samantha. She pulled Jessie onto her lap and patted the ground beside her for Justin to sit.

Kelsie stood on the other side of Samantha for a long minute, looking at the river. Then she sat down with a heaving sigh.

"That man is an idiot," she said to no one in particular.

"That 'man' is my Dad," Lisa reminded her, none too gently. "He's upset, that's all."

"Well, he oughta learn to cool it."

Deciding the conversation was going nowhere, they all stared quietly into the river. Samantha caught a movement out of the corner of her eye. She rested a hand on Jessie's knee.

"Shhhh," she whispered softly, placing a finger in front of her mouth. She pointed out the otter who had been scared away by all the noise but was now floating a few feet upstream from them. Justin tried to hop up, but Lisa restrained him. "Watch," she said softly.

The otter played for them, almost like he was putting on an act at Seaworld. Swimming back and forth in the water, he ducked under the far bank then emerged ten feet upriver with another rock in his paws. He floated on his back, turning the rock over and over like a shiny rubber ball. Suddenly, he flipped and disappeared.

"Where'd he go?" Justin whispered as quietly as a six year old boy could.

"I don't know," Samantha answered. "But maybe if we sit here without making too much noise he'll come back."

"Make him come back, please," Jessie implored.

They waited in silence for the otter's return.

"I guess he decided to go home. Maybe he had dishes to do or something," Samantha said after a few minutes.

Jessie giggled, meeting Samantha's eyes for the first time.

"Jessie! Don't pick that. What'd Grampy tell you?"

"I forgot," said Jessie, twirling a long dead weed through her fingers.

"Grampy tells us and tells us not to pick nothin' in the park, cause the rangers don't like it," Justin explained. "Did he tell you that too, Sammy? I mean Samantha. Can I call you Sammy?"

"Sammy's fine. Samantha's quiet a mouth full, isn't it? Do you want to call me Sammy too?" she asked Jessie.

Jessie shyly nodded her head, then buried her face in Lisa's jacket. Lisa petted her hair as they looked hopefully into the river.

"Sammy, Grampy said you was special," Justin said, facing Samantha as he leaned against a vine covered tree. "How come he said that? Can you stand on your head or touch your elbow to your ear or something?"

Conrad chose that moment to emerge from the woods.

"Whatcha ya'll doin?" he asked as he squatted between Lisa and Samantha. Jessie pushed herself out of Lisa's arms and jumped into Conrad's. "Sorry if I was walking too fast for you to keep up. I had something on my mind, but I'm fine now."

"That's okay, Grampy. We came back here and sat with Sammy. And guess what? We saw an otter. He was swimmin' right there, wasn't he, Sammy?"

"Yep, and tell Grampy what he was doing."

"He was playing with a rock. He was so cute."

Conrad carried Jessie over to the bank. Justin followed, and he grabbed the boy's hand when he got too close to the edge.

"Sorry I missed that," Conrad said. "But I guess we'd better get going. Otherwise we'll be half starved by the time we get to the restaurant."

Justin ran ahead to the van then hopped on one foot while he waited for someone to open the door. Lisa and Kelsie helped the little ones inside, while Conrad and Samantha brought up the rear.

"Sammy, huh?" Conrad said, a true smile breaking across his face for the first time since he broke the unexpected news.

Chapter 13

"What a glorious day," Samantha mentioned to anyone who happened to be listening. She looked up into the pale late autumn sky. There were no signs of the heavy clouds that had come to ground yesterday. Jackets were shed in the mid-day sun, and the kids' colored sweatshirts made bright weaving patterns through the dried grass.

A single tree stood in the field, holding diligently to its few remaining golden brown leaves. A flock of blackbirds swooped up from the field and rested momentarily in its branches. When the kids raced by, the birds flew into the sky almost as one body.

Samantha watched Justin as he ran ahead to the John Oliver cabin, making sure he was the first to reach its porch. Jessie vainly tried to keep up.

"I beat!" Justin yelled back to her, shattering the peace of the cove.

Conrad put a shushing finger to his mouth. "People come up here for quiet, boy, not to listen to you hollering."

Justin took the strong hint, looking around for anyone who he might have disturbed.

"I beat," he stage-whispered to Jessie when Kelsie helped her climb the porch steps.

"Yeah, but I'm prettier," she said back as Conrad had taught her to do when Justin tried to instigate trouble.

The four kids entered the cabin. Justin immediately ran up the short staircase, beckoning everyone to come see.

Samantha stood on the edge of the porch, gazing off at the view of the valley and the mountains beyond. Conrad waited a few feet behind her wishing he was John Oliver; that this was his place and his woman. He longed to stand beside her, his arm around her waist, surveying all that was theirs.

After a few minutes of wistful gazing, she turned without speaking and followed Conrad into the cabin. She noticed the small window that faced the valley below.

Her imagination let her hear John Oliver say, "This is where the winder's gotta be. Does it suit ya?" And of course the wife agreed, as if she had any say in the matter.

She wondered if his wife stayed in awe of these tranquil mountains after she had lived their hardships for a while. Would they seem as beautiful after losing a child to the backwoods ways and lack of a doctor?

When she heard Conrad cough behind her, she turned around, only able to see his outline in the doorway. His features were masked by the sun at his back and she couldn't make out a facial expression.

"I didn't want to interrupt," he said, coming to stand beside her in front of the windows, "but I'm going to take the kids out and let them run a bit. Get rid of a little of that excess energy they've been building up all morning. So, take your time."

And she did. Something called to her and she stood rooted, waiting to hear the message. But nothing came. She finally gave up and walked outside.

Sitting alone on the edge of the porch, Samantha watched Conrad wander around the dirt and grass yard.

"Grampy, come here," Justin called from somewhere out of sight.

Conrad and Jessie followed his voice over to the creek that ran at the edge of the field.

"I didn't never know there was water down here," Justin yelled as they approached.

Samantha bit her tongue as she ignored the double negative, knowing there was time to be a teacher and time to let a kid be a kid.

"This time of year, there's not much water running in it," Conrad told Justin and Jessie. "But come spring, we won't be able to walk on these rocks because the water will be thundering down the mountain after the rains. This is why John Oliver built his house where he did. They needed a steady supply of water for cooking, laundry and Saturday night baths."

"Baths? Yuk," Justin commented, thinking about getting wet and clean in that cold cabin.

Conrad let them hop from rock to rock beside the slow moving creek until Justin almost fell in. Then he led them back up to the field and suggested a game of statue. Lisa and Kelsie joined in, swinging the younger kids around, letting go of their bodies as they fell into frozen positions. Kelsie tried to twirl Justin around cautiously but he was too riled up for that. He egged her on until she spun him around, both feet flying inches from the ground.

"Me too! Me too!" drifted across the meadow as Jessie jumped up and down at Lisa's feet.

"OK, but you've got to be brave."

"I will, Lisy, I promise. Swing me round and round."

Lisa grabbed the tiny hands firmly in hers and began to spin around in slow circles. Jessie's feet flew away from the ground until her Barney shoes showed purple dinosaurs on the bottom. Sounds of her giggling filled the air.

Conrad lowered himself to the grass and sat cross-legged as he watched his family. For the moment, Kelsie seemed like one of them and he was sorry to admit how much he liked that feeling.

Samantha ambled casually toward him and sat a few feet away. He had been running hot and cold all morning. Friendly and casual one minute, sullen and angry the next. He let his eyes rest on her briefly, showing absolutely no emotion, then resumed watching the spinning bodies. As if on cue, they all fell down in a heap, laughing as the world tilted and swayed around them.

Samantha lowered her eyes to the blade of grass she had picked and was slowly shredding. If Conrad wasn't so bullheaded they could be out there having a great time too. She glanced up at him and saw his deep frown as he inspected the gentle peaks rising around them.

No, dammit, I'm done letting him upset me. But why hadn't he told her last night about these children of his? Why did he let her fall head over heels without telling her about his secret life? Why had he so painstakingly kept that from her? He'd had plenty of chances to tell her. When they were strolling down the Parkway, drinking hot chocolate, or even wrapped in each other's arms in the motel doorway. Why had he waited until this morning after she had spent the long sleepless night falling deeper and deeper under his spell? He could have saved them both a lot of heartache if he'd have just...

Her lashes were black with unshed tears when she noticed him get up and cross the field to the mound of bodies. She waited to see if he was going to tell the girls to be more careful with the little ones. Instead he pulled Lisa to her feet, turned her around, grasped his hands together in front of her and started to twirl her around.

"Daddy!" she shouted gleefully as the arc became higher. Dizzily they both tumbled to the ground, Conrad's laughter rang deep and hearty in the autumn sunshine. Soon he was holding Lisa down, tickling the daylights out of her.

Samantha felt she had been invited to a play-back of their early years. Conrad was a good dad and she would have given about anything to have had a father like this for Jeff and Kelsie. She watched Kelsie, wishing there was some way she could turn back the clock and give her this kind of childhood.

Conrad lay on his back, the kids tickling him while he pretended to be no match for them. Kelsie stood aside, wanting desperately to join them, but denying herself the pleasure.

Lisa looked up, her eyes meeting Kelsie's then Samantha's. Conrad chose that instant to try to break away from the grip she had on his shoulders.

"Come on, you guys. Help us."

Kelsie walked forward slowly and half-heartedly held his arm down so the others could tickle his rib cage.

Conrad didn't sense Samantha's approach and was laughing too hard to feel her untie his shoe and ease it off his foot. But he did feel the cool air when she removed the sock. Bucking his foot he tried to tear it away from her grasp. She held it firmly under her arm tickling the tenderest portion at the arch, her back to him.

That was her first mistake. Before she knew what hit her she was flat on her back with a passel of kids and one overgrown boy tormenting every tickle spot that could decently be reached. She tried to wriggle away, twisting her hair and body in the tall grass but it was no use. They had her and they weren't about to let her get away.

Soon they were all breathless and fell off her one by one in exhaustion. Conrad was the last to go and the others watched them as they rolled around on the ground, laughing hilariously.

"Come on, Mom." Kelsie reached down for Samantha's hand. "Get up. Let's go get something to drink. I'm dying of thirst." Her voice was petulant and the others stopped watching Samantha and Conrad to stare at her.

Samantha let herself be pulled up. As they started walking towards the road she turned to Conrad who was still catching his breath on the ground. Though panting wildly, an ear to ear grin split his face. Leaping up he chased her yelling and screaming to the road. They had the back open and the cooler out before the others reached them. Samantha pulled twigs and dried grass out of her curly hair while Conrad passed around cans of soda.

When he handed Kelsie hers she muttered, "Thanks," and turned away sullenly. She sat alone on a big rock at the edge of the field until Lisa strolled over to keep her company.

"Not today, next time maybe," Conrad said when Justin bugged him to stop at the Primitive Baptist Church. He remembered well how antiquatedly beautiful the church was inside, but he also knew about the inevitable trip to the small cemetery that surrounded it. The thoughts of all the little babies that were buried there forced him to keep to the main road. Even the mystery of the cove resident "Murdered by a Carolina rebel" wasn't enough to draw him down that road today.

He noticed Samantha watching him, reading his thoughts once again. Would she never learn to mind her own business? She rested a hand on the top of his knee. He flicked it away and gave her a stony look. Don't, his eyes warned though his mouth remained closed.

He had to slam on the brakes when the car in front of him stopped suddenly. Beside the road stood a herd of deer, their bodies small and compact compared to the corn-fed ones Samantha and Kelsie often saw in Michigan.

"It never fails to amaze me how people go crazy over a deer. I guess I've seen so many that they don't faze me anymore. But some of these people, from New York city and the like, get excited when they even see one of the cows wander close to the fence."

"I still like to see them," Conrad protested. "We'll lose them all someday if we keep on the way we are. Then people will have to go to zoos or parks like this one to see them."

"I wanna see a bear," Jessie piped up from the back seat.

"Me too," everyone else chimed in, all agreeing that would add a special spark to their day.

"Yeah, Conrad. Let's see you conjure up a bear for us." Samantha smiled, looking past him and out his window.

"Okay, I'll try." He scrunched his face up, concentrating hard, as if wishing could make it so. Then he smiled warmly at Samantha before saying, "Done. Just keep your eyes open and wait."

The rest of their trip around the loop was spent looking vainly for one of the black bears that often appeared.

Chapter 14

When they walked in the door of the "Smoky Mountain Junction" restaurant, there was a flurry of excitement as the hostess and two waitresses rushed up to greet Conrad and his family. One waitress, a bleached blonde, waited until the rest had left before waltzing up to Conrad, completely ignoring the rest of the group.

"Hey, Conrad. Where ya been? I was just thinking about you the other day. You know, sorta missing you."

She winked and pressed her body suggestively against his, walking her fingers slowly up and down the middle buttons of his shirt.

Samantha wanted to go over and slap the woman's hands away. How dare this bimbo do something she couldn't even work up the nerve to do? She stopped herself after the first step, reasoning with her head, for a change. She had no hold on him and no right to say or do anything to stop this female Attila the Hun, even knowing that plundering was exactly what she had in mind.

Conrad tried to back away from the body length touches. The blonde pursued him until it became comical to everyone but Conrad and the hussy.

"It's...um...nice to see you again, Esther. Uh...Samantha, come on over here and meet Esther. Esther, this is my very special friend, Samantha," he said, highlighting the 'very' with his voice.

Razor blades so palpable she could almost feel their honed edges penetrated the air between the two women. Samantha extended her hand.

Esther only glared at it. "Charmed, I'm sure," she managed to spit between clenched teeth. "See ya around, Conrad." She turned on her heel and strutted towards the kitchen door, the sway of her hips exaggerated to be sure he and everyone else in the place knew every little bit of what he was missing.

Conrad pulled his hanky out of his back pocket and wiped the perspiration from his face.

"Samantha, I never..." But she had already turned away. He watched her shoulders shake as she made her way to a large table in the corner and sat down. Wondering if Esther's little assault had upset her, he hurried over to her and laid his hand on one of her shoulders then bent over the other. "You okay?" He gently squeezed her shoulder and tried to look into her eyes but she averted her head. Coming around to her side, he sunk down on his haunches. "Samantha?"

Slowly Samantha turned to look at him but the tears in her eyes were not from anger or sadness. They danced on the rims of her eyelids as a raucous laugh escaped her mouth.

Conrad stood as the rest of the crowd started laughing along with Samantha.

"Women!" he muttered as he moved to his seat between Justin and Jessie.

A different waitress came to take their order. This one didn't know Conrad from Adam and was only friendly in a "get a better tip" way.

"I want this kid's "Fun Time" meal," Justin announced, pretending to read from the menu. "You know, chicken legs and biscuits and all that good stuff. And a glass of Coke."

"Milk," corrected Conrad.

"Chocolate milk," corrected Justin.

The waitress next turned her attention to Lisa who was helping Jessie figure out what she wanted.

"Oh geez, I almost forgot. I need a nice big bowl of peas 'cause I love peas, don't I Grampy?"

"You better, boy," Conrad answered between his teeth, never looking up from behind his menu.

Samantha looked back and forth between the two of them wondering what in the world would make peas so important to a six year old.

They ordered their lunches, then sat back to wait. Kelsie and Lisa were in deep conversation, whispering and giggling about the boy/man they had run into out in the cove. He worked at the store there and Lisa knew him from school. They were trying to figure out a way to stop back there after lunch. They'd decided to ask him if he wanted to get together tonight after they got back to town. Lisa figured she'd tell her dad that she'd meant to buy something, maybe a Christmas present, but that she'd forgotten about until now. Maybe he could be conned, maybe he couldn't. They glanced furtively around the table to see if they'd been overheard.

Samantha was deep in conversation with Justin and Jessie. They talked about the train engine that waited in the yard, drawing kids as magnetically as static cling. The track was only six feet longer than the engine but the imaginary journeys went on for miles. The fact that the caboose sat in front of the engine didn't occur to them.

Conrad wasn't paying any attention to the girls' conversation. He sat motionless, his taut muscles denying his relaxed pose. He remembered coming out here with Abby, Jim and the kids at least two or three times a summer. His eyes traveled around the dining room. Nothing had changed. The pictures of antique trains still covered the walls.

On the front wall, between two huge windows hung a large painting of an old train. Five people with a definite family resemblance were climbing up into the coach. The costumes were pure valley country but it was the faces that haunted him. For they most certainly were Lisa, Abby, Jim, Justin and Jessie. He had painted this a year ago last June. The kids had grown restless in their homespun clothing, but the painting had turned out well.

Last Spring he'd brought it out here and donated it to the restaurant in appreciation for all of the good times his family had enjoyed there. Now it called to him, causing intense pain and soothing comfort at the same time.

"Excuse me," he said, standing up suddenly. Curious faces watched as he slowly crossed the room.

"Hey, I know where you're going. Come on, you guys. Come see what my Grampy made." Justin jumped up and followed Conrad. They all left the table and stood behind Conrad and Justin.

"Oh," escaped from Justin's throat, his excitement forgotten. Conrad reached down and tenderly picked him up. Lisa rested her head against her Dad's shoulder, melancholy filling her eyes.

"Remember how happy we were the day I sketched this painting? You guys were antsy as all get out to shed those outfits."

"They were real itchy," Justin said. His head rested on Conrad's chest then whispered, "I miss them, Grampy." Tears misted his voice.

"Me too, Justy. Me too."

"I wanna see," Jessie said pulling at the bottom of Conrad's sweatshirt. Samantha picked her up and held her in front of the painting.

"Is that me, Grampy?"

Conrad's eyes and mind were glued to the painting so Samantha answered. "Yes, honey, that's you. Do you remember when Grampy painted this?"

"Nope. But that's Justy so it's gotta be me too, huh? There's Lisy. See you, Lisy? There's Mommy and Daddy too." She looked around as if she expected them to walk up behind her. "Mommy and Daddy aren't here anymore. Did you know they're up in heaven, Sammy?"

"Yes, Jessie. Grampy told me. I bet you miss them."

"She don't remember them too pretty good. Sometimes I tell her about them so's she won't forget. She was awful little when they..." Justin spoke from where his head lay against Conrad's collarbone.

"I know, Justy." She reached forward and ran her fingers over his silky blond hair. Her fingertips brushed against Conrad's shirt and she carefully withdrew it.

Kelsie poked Samantha's ribs then pointed at the waitress trying to catch their attention. Cold drinks and plates of hot food waited for them.

"Dinner's here," Samantha said. "Let's go eat before it gets cold. Then we can go back out and play on the train some more."

Justin squirmed out of Conrad's arms, reaching for Lisa's hand as his feet hit the floor. Samantha handed Jessie to Kelsie and said quietly, "We'll be right there."

"Conrad?" She waited for him to answer. He continued to stare at the picture, memories assaulting his mind. She decided it was best to leave him be and with a lingering, gentle brush of her hand across the tight muscles of his back she returned to the table. Once there she helped the kids with their chicken drumsticks, biscuits, and coleslaw. Justin dove right into his peas and soon they had all disappeared.

Conrad broke out of his trance and looked around the room. He made his way back slowly and took his place across from Samantha. She used her foot to rub his shin under the table.

"Look, Grampy, I ate all my peas. None rolled on the floor or nothin'." Justin nudged Conrad's elbow, trying to get his attention.

Conrad looked distractedly at him, until his mind caught up with the significance of what he'd heard.

"Good job, Justin. I knew you could do it." A secret smile passed between them.

Conrad pulled himself up into the cab of the ancient train.

"Okay, come on up."

Justin climbed in and sat on Conrad's lap bringing his eyes just above the top instrument panel. He craned his neck to see the horizon in front of him.

"Grampy, I can see the top of the motel across the street now. I never could see that before. I growed, didn't I."

"Yep. By next year I bet you won't even need me as a pillow."

"Next stop Chattanoogie. All aboard."

Jessie pulled on the whistle rope which had long ago been disconnected. "Toot, toot" she yelled above Justin and Conrad's "Chugga, chugga, chugga."

"Ouch! Um, Conrad?" Kelsie began, rubbing the spot on her knee that Lisa's foot had just connected with. They sat at a picnic table eating soft-serve ice cream cones. "I forgot to buy something for my brother out at that gift shop in the cove. Do you think we could run back out there?"

"Kelsie, it's a long way," Samantha began. "What's so important that you can't buy it back in Gatlinburg?"

Lisa and Kelsie looked at each other.

"It was a book, wasn't it Kelsie?" Lisa's nod prompted Kelsie to agree.

"Yeah. Yeah, that's it. A book about music in the cove. You know how much Jeff likes music and I figured this would..."

"Kelsie, you know as well as I do that Jeff couldn't care less about mountain music. Now what gives?"

"You girls must think we're deaf as well as senile," Conrad said. "I heard you talking about Jeb Tate's boy on the way out here, not to mention that little discussion before we ate. What do you say we compromise? I'll drive you back out there and you can shop for a half hour while the rest of us walk around outside. After that I have something I wanted to show everybody anyway. Okay?"

Lisa's "Dad, I'd hoped..." quickly turned into, "Sure, that'll be fine" when she saw his face fix with determination.

Chapter 15

Back in the cove the mountains surrounded them, their soft peaks rising starkly against the blue sky. Samantha had never stopped at this turn out before, hadn't even noticed it. There didn't seem to be any buildings or anything to call Conrad's attention to this pretty little field, but he stopped and got out. After stretching to move around his dinner he walked to Samantha's door.

"Coming?"

"Sure, but..."

"You'll see," was all he would say, although his smile seemed more sincere than it had all day.

As they walked along, Samantha let her imagination run free. She pretended this cove was their homestead. This was her family and they were going out searching for just the right pine tree to decorate their cabin, one not so big that it would fill their small space, but big enough for the burlap angel she had made and starched for the top. The popcorn and cranberries were strung and waiting. Bright red mittens were knitted and wrapped in old newsprint. Venison-vegetable soup simmered on the hearth and homemade wholewheat bread was in the warming oven. Their hand-made clothes were worn but clean, the scuffed shoes handed down from one child to another.

Mothers and Grandmothers always did what was best for the family back then. They never had chances to do what they wanted. She wondered if they yearned for something else. Did they daydream about another life as she was doing now? Were they content as she had never been? Her thoughts grew uncomfortable and she forced herself to stop the silly fantasy.

Conrad turned as they reached the woods. He seemed to be looking for something in particular between the trees. They all followed curiously. When he finally stopped, they looked to see what it was he saw. Only Lisa and Samantha were able to figure it out.

"It's his painting," Lisa whispered reverently to Kelsie.

The scene Conrad had so painstakingly reproduced in his latest painting lay before them, right down to the darkened, withered apples. The only thing missing was the sparkling, bone-chilling layer of hoarfrost. Samantha drew a shaky breath. She brought her camera to her eyes, then futilely knew it would never even come close to Conrad's depiction. A mere photograph could never begin to relay the beauty he had brought to this scene.

"It's as wonderful as your painting," she said as she stood at Conrad's side.

He muttered an unintelligible answer, trying to block thoughts of her watching him paint from his mind. The promises those moments had held seemed miles away now and he grieved for their absence. This scene would forever be marred by thoughts of her standing beside him. The electrical charge that had seemed to pass between them was now expected to fizzle into nothingness.

Samantha raised her camera and took a shot of the four children playing tag in the meadow. This in itself may prove to be priceless. Then she turned the camera on Conrad hoping for a picture to have blown up to life-size so she could hang it beside her bed.

"Nope," he said putting his hand in front of her lens. "Either you have me to look at in the flesh, or you don't have me at all."

He turned away and went out to play with the kids, always mindful to keep his back to her.

Eventually, she set the camera down and stretched out in the warm afternoon sunshine, her mind conjuring up visions of Conrad in the flesh.

She must have dozed. Waking, she found Conrad sitting beside her, leaning across the top half of her body. She could have sworn that she'd felt the silky brush of his lips on hers, but it must have been wishful thinking. There was no sign of it on his face. After releasing her eyes from his, she looked around for the children. They were playing in the apple tree thirty yards away. Dark storm clouds gathered low on the western horizon.

"Time to go," he said barely above a whisper. "It's gonna storm in a bit. Slippery roads scare the tar out of these kids since they heard stories of how their folks died. Let's get them back to the van and high-tail it for home. Maybe we can beat it." Conrad pulled her to her feet then let her fingers drop to her side.

They reached the van just as the first raindrops plopped on the dry grass. Jessie and Justin piled into the middle seat and sat with death grips on each other's hands. Their eyes were panic stricken as they watched Conrad. It grew darker and darker as he drove slowly down the long, winding road. Thunder that had been rolling in the distance now crackled loudly above them. Lightening eerily lit the sky for brief seconds. Soon rain pelted the windows from all sides. Tears streamed down Jessie's face first. Seconds later Justin silently joined her.

Samantha unbuckled her seat belt and crawled over the seat to where the children sat.

"Mind if I join you?" They made room for her between them. "Storms are pretty scary, huh? Hey, I know a story. Maybe if I tell it out loud, I'll forget about the rain and the storm. Have you guys ever heard about the fairy princess and the flying squirrel?"

She made up the story as she went along, telling them of the beautiful princess and the hard working squirrel who wanted to fly. Before long the tears had stopped as they became mesmerized by the tale, only occasionally making sidelong glances out the windows. They listened intently and soon the crooning of her voice lulled them to sleep. Even Kelsie and Lisa napped in the back seat.

Conrad watched and listened. Thoughts of the future tore his heart apart. He caught her eyes in his rearview mirror. She met his gaze steadily, without so much as a hint of commitment.

Chapter 16

There was nothing to be said when they pulled into the motel parking lot. Conrad tugged his coat tight around his waist and walked them to their door. The rain had let up for the time being but the clouds remained low and threatening. Kelsie said a quick goodbye then went into the motel room, turning on the heat first then the TV. The sounds of a commercial for The Dixie Stampede came blaring through the door, distracting them from reality for a few seconds.

Samantha crossed her arms below her breasts. Conrad couldn't tell if the rejecting stance was because of the temperature drop or due to her feelings about him.

"I'm right sorry about the decorations," he said. "I don't remember who told me they were all decked out, but obviously they didn't know what they were talking about."

"That's okay. The cove doesn't need fancy ornaments to be beautiful. I had a good time anyway. Thanks."

Did you, Conrad wanted to ask but decided against it. He took a deep breath and said, "You're more than welcome."

Silence extended the gulf between them.

"Well, I guess I'll go." Please say stay, he didn't add.

She lowered her eyes to the cement at their feet. To where they had first stood together, could it have been less than twenty four hours ago? Beg me not to go, part of her wanted to scream.

When she didn't say anything, he glared at her for a long, uncomfortable second before turning to leave. "See ya," he said, refusing to look back.

Samantha couldn't accept this anger. She ran after him and tried to twirl him around. He locked his arm and legs and stood his ground. Hanging on to his coat she moved around in front of him, forcing him to face her.

"Do you think it's easy for me to let you go like this?" she asked holding his face in her hands. The fluffy softness of his beard distracted her for a moment. She forced herself to go on. "Do you think I like being the bad guy? That I don't care and this isn't hurting me? Well, you're wrong. It never was a question of my not caring. Never!" Tears choked off her voice and streamed down her face.

Conrad's eyes followed their path as they dripped off her chin. How his lips longed to follow them when they hit her coat above her breasts. Instead he wiped his thumbs across the streaks on her cheeks, interrupting their flow.

"I know you care," he said, looking through her eyes and into the deepest regions of her soul. Barely above a whisper he sadly added, "Just not enough." He turned and walked down the path to his family.

Samantha stared at the spot where he had stood until well after he was gone. A strong northerly wind picked up but it was many minutes before she would move. The door opened behind her then closed almost as silently. A violent shiver racked her body, whether it was from the bitter cold or the pain of his going she couldn't tell. She trembled again as she walked back to the room, composing her face so Kelsie wouldn't know how bad she was hurting.

"I had fun today. Did you?" Kelsie lay on her stomach crosswise on the bed. She turned her head away from the television to look at her mother. "Mom?"

"Yes, Kelsie, it was a good day." Her voice said the words, but her eyes and heart were closed.

"I'm sorry, were you sleeping?"

Samantha opened her eyes. What did Kelsie expect from her now? Couldn't she tell she only wanted to be left alone?

"What I'm trying to tell you is that I guess Conrad is all right after all. He seemed kinda weird last night, but today he acted like an okay guy. Lisa thinks he's cool and those grandkids of his think the sun rises and sets on his say so."

Samantha continued to stare. Everything Kelsie said was true. But in the morning they would leave and that would be the end of it.

"So if you want to see more of him, and you can take that anyway you want, it's tolerable to me. Good Lord, where did 'tolerable' come from? Lisa. I guess these folks are rubbing off on me."

"Well, don't make it a habit." The words snapped out, angry and bitter. "We're leaving for home first thing in the morning, just like we'd planned. You should be happy that we'll never see any of these 'folks' again. You might as well forget about them. It was fun, now it's over. End of story. No more pages. No more chapters. The end." She got up and went into the only room where she could have privacy, slamming the door behind her.

Conrad fixed bologna sandwiches for supper. Everyone tried so hard to be helpful that by the time the meal was over, they were all tired and impatient. He rushed the kids through their baths and tucked them in for the night.

"Grampy?" came Justin's call across the room just before Conrad turned out the light.

"Yeah?"

"I like Sammy. She's real nice"

"Me too, Grampy," Jessie added.

"Me too, kids". Flicking the light off, he quickly left the room. "Me too."

He stood in the hallway, leaning into the forearm that was raised over his head against the wall, a gesture of utter defeat. Lisa walked up behind him and rubbed her hand slowly between his shoulders.

"Women are slime, huh Dad?"

"Sure, Lisa. Women are slime." He said goodnight and went in his room. This promised to be the first of many long, lonesome nights to come.

"Mom?" Kelsie said through the bathroom door. "I'm going to run down to Mickey D's and get us some burgers. I'll be back in a few minutes. Mom? Mom, did you hear me?"

"Yes, Kelsie, I heard you. Be careful," Samantha yelled back over the noise of the shower. She waited until Kelsie closed the door before she let go of the tears that had been building most of the day. Pain ripped through her chest. She stopped sobbing long enough to wonder if she could be having a heart attack. No such luck. It was only her heart tearing in two. Half she would take back to Michigan and half would always be here with a southern mountain man who had entranced her so completely in such a short time.

Chapter 17

That night, when the lights were out and Kelsie was snoring softly in the bed beside her, memories of the emotions she had felt the night before kept Samantha wide awake. Conversations with herself bickered through her mind.

"So what would be so bad about staying here with Conrad?" she asked her alter ego.

"What do you mean? You know you've got things to do, places to go, people to see," she answered.

"But maybe he's the Mr. Right I've always dreamed of."

"How could he be with those two little kids to take care of…forever."

"But they're good kids. They wouldn't be much problem."

"Not much problem? They'd take over your whole life."

"Would that be so bad?"

"No but…"

"They really could use a full time 'Grammy'."

"But what about the plans, the 'me' time that's always been just around the corner? The traveling you wanted to do. California, Texas, Maine? The shop near Lake Huron? The Santas and Christmas stuff you wanted to sell? The antiques to refinish? That old house you always wanted to bring back to life? All that will be gone, probably for good this time. Can you live with that?"

"I don't know. I really don't. I've waited my whole life for this time. My chance to do what I want, without worrying about anybody but me. How can he expect me to give that up to become a full-time parent again?"

"Well, he is pretty special...and those eyes...and those lips...and that..."

"Wait a minute. Whose side are you on, anyway?"

"Oh, I forgot."

"Shut up and go to sleep."

Feeling foolish and exhausted from the lack of sleep the night before, Samantha eventually quieted the voices. Shortly before three o'clock she finally slowed the pictures of Conrad reeling through her mind. She wasn't aware of drifting off into a dreamless sleep.

Chapter 18

Conrad stayed up, pacing the inside of the house like a starving mountain panther, only what he was starving for certainly wasn't meat. He was hungry for Samantha, emotionally and physically.

He tried watching television then roamed from room to room. Stopping here to gaze out the window, asking for answers from the rain-darkened pines. Stopping there to do up the supper dishes. At 2:30 he slowly trudged up the stairs to his room. Knowing he was too restless to sleep, he pulled a chair up to the window, braced his feet on the windowsill and sunk deep into thought.

Staring out the window, his injured mind wandered away from the hurt of Samantha leaving to the bad days after Abby had been killed and then back to Samantha. He didn't realize he'd dozed off until a soft pinging sound on the windows woke him up. Pulling his feet down, he sat forward in the chair, trying to clear his eyes and his mind. Frozen raindrops hit the window. He looked down at the ground. A partially hidden moon lit up the scene below. A white layer of snow sparsely blanketed the grass. As he watched big lacy flakes, some the size of quarters, replaced the smaller icy ones.

He turned his bedside radio on WDLY, low so as not to wake the kids. Crossing back to the window, he pulled his chair up and rested his chin on his crossed arms braced on the window sill. He watched as the snow piled up rapidly.

"Surprise!" was what Dolly's weatherman said about the massive snowstorm heading their way. He saw the flakes as literal pennies from heaven, white replacing the traditional copper. If there were enough of them, maybe they would buy him Samantha for a few more days. Time enough to win her over. Time to show her how simple their lives could be. Time. Maybe that's all he needed.

Chapter 19

"Kelsie, wake up! Good Lord, we must've overslept." Samantha bounded out of bed before she could get her bearings, barking her shin on the footboard. "Come on, get moving. We're not even packed yet. We've got to get on the road."

"Huh?" Kelsie mumbled without waking up.

Samantha grabbed her skinned leg with one hand and the travel alarm clock with the other. She looked at its face in the filtered light from the window. Seven thirty? Should it be this bright at 7:30? In November? She shook the clock, wondering if it had died in the night. When she pulled back the curtain to get a better look, the glare of a totally white world assaulted her eyes. Rooftops, driveways, trees; everything in sight was coated with a layer of wintery white. The porch rail held about five inches of snow and it was still coming down. She could barely make out the Space Needle only a block away and the mountains were merely vague outlines on the horizon.

"You're not going to believe this," she said to Kelsie who had pulled the covers over her head to block the brightness. Samantha shook Kelsie's foot. "Hey, come see why I'm going to let you go back to sleep."

"How 'bout if I sleep first, then you show me?"

Samantha gave up and turned on the radio, hoping the scene outside her window was an illusion brought on by lack of sleep.

"This surprise snow covers everything from Lexington to Atlanta," the disc jockey was saying. "Honest folks, they promised me it was going to stay rain. Well, you know the National Weather Service. Might as well enjoy this mess, 'cause it ain't going to get any better for a while. As a matter of fact, by tonight they're talking another nine inches. Yep, you heard me. We're looking at a total of a foot and a half before this is all over. So settle in, fix up a pot of soup and find a good book cause it's going to be a long one." His next selection was, appropriately, Vince Gill's version of "White Christmas". She turned the radio off and gazed out the window again.

Okay, now what? She'd heard about how these freak snowstorms could paralyze the roads and wondered how long they would be stuck here. She'd use up all of her personal days in about a week. Well, she'd have to wait a while before she called Sue at home to tell her she wouldn't be at school for a few days. They'd only have to turn on the Weather Channel to see that she wasn't making it up about being snowed in there in the northern reaches of the sun belt. Then the kennel. Dolly, their yellow lab, would be having a prolonged stay and at ten dollars a day, Samantha hoped she was enjoying herself. She'd have to go to the motel office to see if they could stay. That shouldn't be a problem. She could finish maxing her charge card and maybe get some cash somewhere.

Her thoughts strayed to Conrad but she pushed him back into the recesses of her subconscious.

The muffled knock on the door startled her. It seemed out of place coming from the snow-hushed world outside.

"Probably the motel people," she said to Kelsie who gave no answer. Pulling on her robe, she ran her fingers through her hair. "Yuk," she said, sticking her tongue out as she walked past the mirror on the wall.

When she opened the door there stood Conrad, snow coating his hair and beard. Her heart jumped at how boyishly handsome he looked as he stood knee deep in a snow drift, his ungloved hands shoved deep in his jacket pockets.

"Can you come out and play?" he asked, smiling like a small child blessed by the year's first snowstorm. They stared at each other, neither one wanting to break the spell of the white wonderland.

"Close the door, for crying out loud!" Kelsie bellowed from the bed.

Samantha pulled Conrad into the room by the front of his coat. He stomped his feet and brushed himself off, never taking his eyes off her tousled hair and dumbfounded face.

"We...that is the kids and I...we were wondering if you'd like to come stay at our place. It's supposed to keep snowing all day and get real bad by tonight."

Now he looked at everything in the room but her.

She wondered if this was a good idea. Neither one of them could handle repeating yesterday's scenario. Still, she wanted to go with him more than anything in the whole wacky white world.

"If you're sure we won't be in the way. I wouldn't want to..."

Conrad pulled her to him, glanced at Kelsie to be sure she was faking sleep, then kissed her gently. His lips were cold and wet. "You'll never be in my way."

Samantha watched his eyes. "No commitments, right?" she said hoping they wouldn't be overheard.

"No," he answered gruffly, then softened his tone. "No commitments. Just a good time for everybody. Okay?"

"Well, give us a few minutes to throw things together. Kelsie, get moving."

"Mom, I can't get out of bed with him here."

"I'll wait in the van. You can take a shower or whatever it is you women do in the morning at my place. But hurry, okay? It's already getting a little slick out there."

Chapter 20

Samantha was thankful that Conrad was driving. As they made their way up the winding mountain road, she tried to keep from reaching for the arm rest. Kelsie sat in the next seat back, fists clenched, teeth locked and eyes shut. Occasionally she would peek to see if they were still alive.

"Not too much farther now," Conrad said as they turned on a still narrower road.

"This can't possibly be a two way street, can it?" Samantha asked. "I'll bet it's a lot wider when there isn't any snow. Right?"

Conrad just smiled.

The road wound around the side of a mountain and if anyone was coming from the other direction, there would be no chance of missing them. Luck was with them, or they may have been the only people foolish enough to be out. Samantha watched as the passenger side mirror whisked snow off the mountain side. As they began a second try up the next incline, Kelsie made the mistake of looking behind and seeing how close they were to the drop off at the bottom of the hill. She moaned, then sunk lower yet into the seat, double-checking to make sure her seatbelt was intact. They made it up to the top of the incline only to see another one ahead.

"Now I lay me down to sleep," Kelsie started to chant in the back seat.

Conrad smiled at Samantha, though never taking his eyes off the road.

"Having fun back there?" he asked Kelsie, glancing for the barest of seconds over his shoulder at her.

"Watch the road, Romeo," was all she could answer.

After what seemed like an hour on the treacherous roads they pulled in between two aged stone pillars. An old farmhouse, almost surrounded by ancient pine trees, sat at the end of the drive. It was barely visible through the zillions of snowflakes.

"Pretty," Samantha said as she let her gaze settle on the house. The metal roof cried out for a coat of paint to cover up the rusty areas and she could picture it in red. The white siding of the house looked yellowed against the fresh snow. A wide wrap-around porch covered three sides and slanted almost imperceptively at the far end. Unassuming S-curved gingerbread trim laced all but one of the porch posts. Stark naked lilac bushes infringed on the porch at the front corners. A faded to almost pink cantilevered barn stood across the driveway.

"Yeah, gorgeous. Now can you stop this van?" Kelsie said, her hand on the rear door handle.

Conrad's eager grin was replaced by a deep frown as he noticed Samantha's reaction to the house. He looked at it as he hadn't done in years and was instantly sorry he hadn't gotten around to painting it last summer. He'd meant to, even had the paint in the basement but then, with the kids and all, it completely slipped his mind.

He pulled up even with the side entrance to the porch.

"I sure am glad you're used to driving these crazy roads in this stuff. I would have been a basket case," Samantha said quietly as Conrad shut off the engine.

"Darlin', I don't drive in this stuff. We usually close everything down and stay home. I've never driven on this much snow in all my life. Kinda fun, ain't it?" His smile faltered a bit as he rested his forehead on the steering wheel. After a few seconds, he peeled his clenched fingers from the wheel.

As soon as Samantha could close her mouth she said weakly "Let's get into the house before I choke you to death or something." And how seriously did he mean that 'Darlin' stuff.

"I'll get the bags," Conrad said as he pulled himself together. "Ya'll go on up to the house."

Samantha grabbed what she could then waited at the steps for Conrad to lead the way. She turned this way and that trying to find the mountains, but they were lost in the whitened sky. If it kept up much longer they would be totally snowbound. She felt secluded and was surprised at how good that felt. The word "trapped" filtered through her mind, but she chased it away.

Conrad stomped his feet on the wide porch floorboards.

"Which way are the mountains from here?" Samantha asked as she tried to peer through the snow and into the distance. "I know they must be out there somewhere, but I can't make them out."

"The main range is off in through there" he said pointing to the right of the porch. "We've got almost a 360 degree view from different spots on this place. The 'get rich quick' developers come out at least once a year trying to talk me into selling forty acres from the back of the property. So far I've been able to hold them off."

"Good for you."

"Yeah, well my granddad's father first farmed this land. I can't very well let him down after all that he went through to raise crops in these rocky fields. When the snow's gone, I'll show you the view from the back of the property."

"Hey! Can we go in please? My fingers are already frozen to this suitcase handle." Kelsie's complaint drew both of their minds away from their murky future and back to the present.

Conrad walked across the porch to the door, the heels of his cowboy boots slapping hard on the wooden plank floor.

"Welcome," he said as he pushed the door open, stepping aside to let them in ahead of him. Inside everything was church quiet for about three seconds. Then the house came to life. A door from another room flew open and Jessie and Justin burst through.

Bouncing up and down with excitement Justin said, "Holy cow, is it snowin'! Did you see it, Sammy? Ain't it great? Wanna go sleddin'? Grampy made us sleds out of a great big box. He made them this morning. He was up before Tweety was even on. How come you was up so early, Grampy? I bet he'll make you a sled if you want. You want one too, Kelsie? Wanta go sleddin' too? Huh Sammy? Huh Kelsie? Do ya?"

"Chill, Justin," Lisa said as she joined the group. "Let them get in the door before you ask so many questions."

Jessie had thrown herself at Samantha's legs, hugging them with all the strength in her little arms. Then she ran to the window and stood there for a minute before turning to Samantha with her eyes wide with wonder.

"Snowin'," she said quietly.

Samantha crossed the room and knelt down beside her. "Yep, snowin. Lots and lots. Justin, we better wait a while before we go sledding. Let it pile up real good and it'll be more fun."

"Yeah. Maybe it'll get ten feet high! You think it will, Sammy?"

"We'll just have to wait and see, won't we?" She saw Conrad watching her over Justin's head and tried not to read his mind. Just like Justin, he'd like to see it snow ten feet. Then it would be Spring before she could leave. The thought that maybe it wouldn't be such a terrible thing after all ran unbidden and unwelcome through her mind.

Lisa came over and took Jessie's hand. "Come on guys, let's take their stuff upstairs. Kelsie you can bunk with me unless you think you'll miss your Mom." They laughed about that one all the way to Lisa's room. Jessie and Justin followed close behind, not wanting to miss a bit of their excitement.

Samantha's eyes adjusted to the dim indoor light. The rooms were large, and obviously had not seen a decorative touch for a long long time. Old and faded cabbage rose wallpaper lined the dining room. A sea of worn gray linoleum was tacked to the floor, covered in places by mismatched area rugs. An age-darkened oak buffet stood against the far wall, perfectly matching the huge round table in the center of the room.

Conrad stood beside her. "What can I say? Julia never stayed stay home long enough to take care of the girls, let alone the house.

Lately we've had other things on our minds. We try to keep up, but with the kids and all we didn't have time for Spring cleaning, let alone decorating."

"Conrad, please," Samantha said softly. "It's comfortable. Like coming home to Grandma's or something. I almost expect to see fresh baked bread and homemade jam in the kitchen."

He looked at her to see if she was poking fun at him, but her eyes said she wasn't.

They walked slowly through the rooms, and by the time they reached the kitchen, she had fallen in love with the quaint house. Her mouth dropped open in surprise when Conrad pushed open the swinging door and they entered the kitchen. The walls were a shocking florescent green with no pictures, shelves or domestic paraphernalia to break the brittle harshness.

"This was Julia's one attempt at decorating. I came home one night to find the walls and most of Julia painted this horrible color. She said she was going to paint the cupboards Sunkist orange. I guess I laughed so much that she left the rest of the house alone."

The cupboard doors each had a jagged slash of orange paint running down their length.

"I think maybe you shouldn't have made her mad. Looks like she got a little vindictive."

"Yeah. About that and everything else I said or did." Conrad sighed then ushered her back into the living room.

At a small walnut table near the huge stone fireplace, he showed her the pictures of his mother, grandparents and finally his daughters and grandchildren. As he looked at Abby's picture, the rest of the world receded and he was trapped in the loving smile on his daughter's face.

Samantha wrapped her arms around him from behind and laid her head against the tense muscles of his back. Conrad clutched her hands and they swayed gently from side to side. Sounds of stamped-ing elephants reverberating on the stairs pulled them apart.

"Sometimes they get a little rowdy," he explained, squinting his eyes in dismay. Not for the first time, he wished the kids would take it just a little bit easy. Give Samantha time to slowly get used to them and their ways in the confines of the house before they showed their true colors.

"Now, Grampy? Can we go out now? Looks like there's plenty of snow." Justin ran back and forth from the window to Conrad, anxiously, if not quietly, awaiting his answer.

"I think we better wait 'til it lets up a little. If we went out now we might get separated. We'll have lots of fun later."

"Grampy, you promised," Justin tone turned to a whiny complaint.

"Justin, be patient. Now stop before I give you something to whine about."

Justin stopped, but not from fear of being spanked. His Grampy would never lay a hand on him and he knew it. But he also knew if Grampy got mad, some of the fun would go out of playing in the snow.

"Okay," he said, trying hard to hide the tremble in his lower lip. He turned to Lisa, begging her to find some way to take his mind off the wait.

Chapter 21

The snow piled up as the sky grew darker. By noon the wind picked up, blowing the white powder from patches of nearly bare earth to drifts five foot tall.

While the adults and near adults played a ruthless game of Monopoly at the dining room table, Justin paced back and forth from the window to the game of Cootie he was playing with Jessie. Whenever there was a break between flakes, he would turn his eyes expectantly to Conrad.

"Not yet," Conrad would silently mouth as Justin's face fell again. Soon he gave up the game and went to sit in front of the low multipaned picture window, pressing his nose firmly against the glass. To the untrained eye it would look like he was waiting patiently. Only Conrad could see the excitement wiggling the young boy's ears.

Jessie's Cootie now had four noses in the leg holes and two legs raising crookedly from the antenna holes. She had taken advantage of Justin's distraction to build the Cootie just the way she wanted without following his silly rules. She hopped it around on the rug, twisting and tumbling it in a strange bug dance, then made it attack the perfect one Justin had left behind. But she soon realized it wasn't any fun if he didn't complain. She took her Cootie apart and carefully put the pieces back in the box before she went over to sit beside Justin at the window. Before long she was sound asleep in a ball on the floor.

Conrad quietly excused himself from the game then grabbed the quilt off the back of the couch and tucked it around both children. Justin, who had closed his eyes for a second, looked up expectantly. Conrad shook his head again. Winter's light was beginning to fade from the sky. It was not even supper time yet, but it was already too dark to go out and play in the snow today. Dejectedly he lay down on the quilt next to Jessie and fell asleep.

Conrad flipped the switch on the overhead chandelier and the room was illuminated with its warm glow. He sat back down and smiled at the three females circling him.

"You know, tomorrow we're going to have to take him outside whether this blizzard lets up or not. He's gonna beg and whine 'til we can't stand it."

"Dad," Lisa said and laid her hand on top of his as he fiddled with the steel dog on the gameboard. "I'm just so glad to see him get excited about something." She turned to Samantha and Kelsie. "For months Justin was close to catatonic. He'd sit in front of the TV for hours, doing nothing but staring. One day I turned it off, you know, to see if he'd notice. It was an hour before he complained. Then I thought he'd never stop crying. Poor little guy."

They sat in silence as the light faded around them.
Finally, Samantha cleared her throat and asked, "Lisa, how did you get through those days?" Though speaking to Lisa, her eyes briefly

wandered to Conrad. His body had become board stiff as he leaned back in his chair.

"It was awful," Lisa said, lowering her eyes to her hands as she picked aimlessly at the polish on her nails. "My friends didn't know what to say to me, so they said nothing at all. I almost felt...like I was guilty of something."

Conrad's eyes flashed open and filled with pain. He'd never heard this before and it hurt to hear it now.

"Oh, Sue Ellen called me a couple of times and Mark Knight, who I've known since kindergarten, came by to see me once, but he never came back. I understand that it was because they didn't know how to help, but at the time I was so angry and I felt like nobody cared."

"Lisa, I..."

"I know Dad, you did the best you could. You tried, but you were hurting as bad as I was. After I found out how Mom felt about me, there didn't seem to be much sense in going on."

A shudder ran through Conrad's body. Samantha watched it but returned her attention to Lisa. Sitting alone in the living room that afternoon he'd told her the story of the nightmare evening when Lisa had walked in on his and Julia's fight.

"I can't imagine how bad that must have been," Samantha said as she got up and walked around the table to Lisa. She rested her hands on the trembling shoulders. Lisa flinched at the touch, then relaxed into Samantha's fingers as they kneaded her tensed muscles.

"I know I'm an outsider here," Samantha began.

Lisa grabbed her fingers and gave them a brief squeeze as Conrad closed his eyes.

"But I'm sure your Mom loves you as well as she knows how."

"Yeah, sure. Like I love the stomach flu."

"You've got to realize that it's her problem. She's selfish and shallow and deserves your pity, not your hatred. She's the one who's screwed up, honey, not you."

Lisa twisted in her chair until her eyes met Samantha's. "Do you think so? Do you really think it's Mom's fault?" Hope filled her eyes as she stood up.

Samantha pulled her into her arms and held her close. "Let's go upstairs for some girl talk. I think it's time we talked about some of the most important facts of life."

Kelsie stood up to follow, then sat back down when Samantha waved her away.

Chapter 22

Conrad's eyes opened when he heard Kelsie clearing the Monopoly board from the table.

"I thought you were sleeping," she said.

"No, thinking is all." He smiled crookedly then added, "Looks like it's up to you and me if anybody is going to get anything to eat around here tonight. Are you game?"

"Sure. I make a pretty mean grilled cheese sandwich if you've got soft butter and sliced cheese. Otherwise, forget it." She followed him into the kitchen.

"I was thinking maybe tacos. That sound okay to you?. I'll make my special taco meat and you can cut up the vegetables. Did you ever see blue taco shells?" he asked as he pulled some out of the refrigerator.

They bantered back and forth as they prepared the meal. The sizzle and aroma of frying ground beef, onions and peppers filled the kitchen. After Kelsie diced the tomatoes she laid her knife down and went to Conrad's side. He had fallen silent again.

"Mom's pretty good at this...making people feel better, I mean."

"Shouldn't I have sensed she was having problems? I thought everything was finally going well. Guess maybe we do need a woman's touch around here, and for more than decorating."

"Hey, don't beat yourself up about not understanding Lisa. Maybe it's just a female thing. You know, like PMS or something. Maybe Mom can be persuaded to hang around to help out. She loves a challenge."

"Yeah, maybe." Silence descended again but not as darkly as before. "Thanks, Kels. You're not so bad for a teenager."

"Well, you're not so bad for an old man either. And your 'Conrad's special meat' is burning."

Half an hour later Kelsie woke the children then hollered up the stairs that supper was ready. Lisa's eyes were puffy when she placed her arms gently around Conrad's neck.

"I love you, Daddy," she said after kissing his cheek. Leaving him smiling, she grabbed a sleepy tyke under each arm and manhandled them into their chairs.

Kelsie and Samantha huddled at the bottom of the stairs, whispering quietly. When they finished, Samantha put her arm around Kelsie's shoulder and together they walked into the dining room.

"Look at Conrad's special recipe for tacos," Kelsie said when they reached the table. "Chili beans. Isn't that a great idea?"

Samantha caught her wink and returned one. They had used Conrad's secret ingredient for years but neither one would tell him that. His faced beamed as they all filled their shells and complimented him on his wonderful cooking.

They ate tacos 'til they were coming out their ears. Yet two hours later when Conrad mentioned popcorn, they were all ready, willing and able to help get the supplies around. Conrad stoked up the fire while Justin ran for the fireplace popper hanging from a nail near the back door. Lisa helped Jessie dig out the big pink crockery bowl from under the cupboard.

"Wow, popcorn without a microwave. Will wonders never cease?" Kelsie said as she started melting butter in a saucepan. Samantha followed Conrad's instructions for how much Crisco to bring in for the popper.

They sat on the floor, forming a half circle around Conrad as the corn began pinging against the metal box. Justin kept inching forward to keep a closer eye on the popper then sliding back as the heat became too intense for his tender skin. The sounds in the popper became dull thuds as it filled with popped corn.

Conrad dumped the corn into the bowl and Kelsie carefully poured the melted butter over each piece. Lisa helped Jessie add salt until Conrad said "enough."

Trying to prove to Samantha that they had couth in this house, he had brought in bowls for each of them. But before he could fill a single bowl, everyone had a hand in the big one.

"Alright, I know when I'm licked," he said good naturedly laughing as he reached in and got a handful for himself.

Chapter 23

"Samantha, I..." Conrad started. The kids had gone up to bed and the two of them were left in the room lit only by the dying embers in the fireplace. Samantha lay stretched out on her side on the rug, her left arm pillowing her head. Conrad sat on the floor beside her. Leaning against the couch, he watched the fire, trying to find the right words to tell her how important it was to him that she was here. When he looked down at her, he saw her eyes were closed. "Are you asleep?" he asked a little more loudly than was necessary.

Samantha lay still, silently faking sleep, trying to breathe in and out evenly. No matter what it was he was about to say, she didn't want to deal with it. Professions of love or manifestations of guilt...neither one appealed to her tonight. Tonight was for relaxation and letting sleeping dogs lie. So that was exactly what she did; lay there, well aware of his eyes as they traveled across the hills and valleys of her body. Opening her eyes to slits, she watched him suspiciously as he approached her, wondering what he had in mind. He stooped to place his arms under her legs and shoulders, moaning softly as he lifted her dead weight into his chest.

Still faking she put her arms around his shoulders, figuring she couldn't be held responsible for something she did when she was sound asleep. She curled into his shoulder and buried her nose into his smoky shirt.

Conrad carried her up to the guest room, the one that had been his grandparent's years before. It was the same as his Mamaw had left it; yellow and white chenille bedspread, small yellow tea roses on a striped wallpaper, hardwood floors, even the hooked rug beside the bed was the same, though faded from years of sunshine that flowed into the room from the two large windows.

Samantha had left the bedside lamp on and its soothing glow made the room warm, inviting and sensual. He laid her gently on the bed, trying not to wake her, even though he wasn't one hundred percent sure she was actually asleep.

She let him take her slippers off, wondering what she would do if he started to remove more. All of the romance novels she'd ever read with such encounters ran through her head, but in most of them the female had been either drunk or injured. Surely, he wouldn't be so bold as to undress her for bed. And would she continue to fake sleep if he did? Maybe. Maybe not. She fought not to smile at the thought.

Conrad watched her in the soft light. He realized he walked a fine line between the propriety of what he knew was necessary and the indecency of his desires. With a shrug of his shoulders, he pulled the covers from the other side of the bed over her bluejeaned legs. Grabbing a spare blanket from the closet, he covered her body and tucked it gently under her chin. He thought he felt a flutter of movement when he kissed her cheek, but decided it didn't matter now anyway.

"Goodnight, Darlin'," he whispered as he closed the door, then went to his own bed, alone again as it seemed he had been most of his life in one way or another.

"Goodnight, sweet prince," Samantha whispered to the empty room.

Chapter 24

Justin barged into Conrad's room as soon as daylight filtered through the blinds.

"It stopped, Grampy," he said, pouncing up and down on the bed, bare feet just missing various parts of Conrad's lower anatomy. "Can..we go..out and..play...now? Please?." His timbre of his voice rose and fell with his body.

"Please, Grampy, please. See? I'm all dressed and ready to go," Jessie said.

Through sleep-filled eyes Conrad peered at the little girl standing near the bed. She wore her flannel nightgown, bunny slippers, Sunday coat and the straw hat Ada wore in the garden. Trying to focus on the form as it bounced, he turned his eyes to Justin who was much better prepared in his striped pajamas, bare feet and Lisa's florescent pink ski jacket that hung seven inches past his fingertips.

"Come on..get a..move on..time's a..wastin'..let's go..before it all..melts." Justin hopped down to the side of the bed nearest to Conrad's head. "Hurry up."

"Hold your horses. Give me a minute to wake up, will ya? Go downstairs and look in the closet for those mittens we found yesterday while I get dressed."

"Okay, Grampy, but we don't trust you. Grab hold, Jessie." Jessie ran to the top of the bed, across from Justin. Each child grabbed a corner of the bedding and stripped it down the sides until it lay in a heap on the floor at the foot of the bed. Conrad bounded up suddenly and chased them running and screaming from the room.

"Holy cow, did we get the snow," he said to himself as he looked out the window, trying to figure out how to dress for the coming day outside. "Samantha's here," he added as a smile lit his face.

He finished tucking his flannel shirt into his jeans as he walked down the stairs, remembering to zip up before he ran into anybody unfamiliar with his casual ways. As he neared the bottom step he saw Samantha crouching in the corner of the dining room and stopped himself before he stepped on the stair that always creaked. He watched her as she carefully pulled the loose linoleum away from the floor.

"Oak," he heard her say, though it was barely above a whisper. He coughed to let her know he was coming, then finished walking down the steps.

She stood up to meet him, a sheepish grin pulling at the corners of her mouth.

"I'm sorry. I've been doing a little snooping. This is really an incredible old house. With a little work you could..."

He looked at her, then at the water-stains on the wallpaper and the dust bunnies under the buffet.

"Yeah, it looked good when my grandparents lived here. We stayed with them for a while 'til Papaw told Mom she'd either quit drinking or find somewhere's else to live. I think that's what they call 'tough love' nowadays. Anyway, that's when we moved up the road a piece to a little three room shack. It was all she could afford, and still have enough money for her booze. You wouldn't believe how cold that place got in the winter."

He stopped talking and walked slowly around the room, running a hand along the top of the chair rail. Julia had threatened to paint the wainscoting hot pink, but luckily she had lost interest before she found the perfect hideous shade.

"This is oak too," Conrad said, trying to polish up the table with his hanky. "Mamaw kept it shined so well you could see the light reflect from it." He looked up at the cut glass chandelier that hung over the table. Dust webs that hadn't been visible the night before ran from prism to prism and back up to the base of the lamp. "She'd be pretty disappointed in the way I've let this place go. Ada tries, bless her heart, but there's just too much."

"Hey, you're not superman," Samantha said from his side. "What's important is the people who live here, not the house itself. Besides, all it needs is a little sprucing up. If Julia had been a 'Susie

Homemaker', you'd probably be dealing with 70's gold brocade wallpaper and brown shag carpet. Yuk!"

He watched the faked shiver run through her body, then reached out and pulled her close to him. Suddenly he clamped his mouth over hers to keep from saying how she could fix the place up any way she liked, if she'd only stay.

The sounds of wild Indians swooping down the stairs pulled them apart. Two half-asleep teenagers followed the younger children. This time everyone was dressed for the cold weather.

"Breakfast first," Samantha insisted but even Conrad deserted her.

"Come on! We can eat later," Conrad whined. "Let's go play before it all melts."

Samantha gave him a dirty look, then pulled her coat from the coat-tree by the door. Justin was outside and bounding through the piles of snow before Conrad could even get his boots laced.

Chapter 25

Sunlight flooded the glittering field beside the house, its glare blinding them as they fished their sunglasses out of their pockets.

"Be careful not to track up all the snow," Justin warned them all gravely. Conrad's laughter echoed off the trees and mountains.

"Boy, you couldn't track up all this stuff in three weeks." It was almost a foot and a half deep and crunched loudly under their feet.

"Don't put me down yet," Jessie said from her perch in Conrad's arms. "I...I'm afraid."

"I won't let you go, honey." He walked carefully so he wouldn't slip and send them both to the ground. Finding a spot under an ancient pine tree where the snow wasn't quite as deep, he nonchalantly sat down with a plop.

Jessie tightened her grip on Conrad's neck then laughed out loud at the white fluff that billowed up around her. She swished her mittened hands back and forth through the snow then licked some off her mitten.

"Is it like ice cream?" Conrad asked as he scooped some up to eat.

"Nope. Cold but not sweet or chocolaty or nothin'."

"Grampy, it won't pack." Justin moaned as he trudged up to Conrad. "Look, it keeps falling apart. Make it pack. Please." He squeezed some snow in his mittened hand then let it drop to the ground, disappointed that it was so powdery.

"It's still too cold. We need it to warm up a little before it'll pack good. Then we'll make that snow man you've been nagging about. For now, you'll have to be content to play in it."

He set Jessie on her feet then stood up, brushing the snow from the back of his jeans. After making sure Jessie was okay, he scooped up an armful of snow and threw it in the air above Justin's head.

Justin did a little dance in the cloud of snow as it tumbled around him.

"Me, Grampy, me," Jessie shouted as she jumped up and down at Conrad's side until he scooped up a smaller armful and carefully let it drift over her. She caught her breath, wondering if she should be afraid of the white flakes billowing around her shoulders. Her laughter, when she decided that's what she should do, bounced all around the valley.

Samantha stood apart from the frolicking bunch, gazing almost reverently at the view. In the clear morning air, she could see the mountain peaks in the distance. Covered with a white downy blanket, sharp spikes of hunter green and black emerged through the fuzz.

She walked to the top of a nearby slope and looked up the wooded hillside. Where the trees were dense, the ground was almost snowless.

Conrad handed Jessie off to Kelsie and silently crept up behind Samantha, bent on tackling her, but as he drew closer something in her stillness made him stand quietly beside her, trying to see something he might have missed for the past 46 years. Even the painter in him had ignored this view in favor of other, more remote places. He tried to envision what he could do to make this scene special. Deep down he knew but his mind skimmed over the ache it caused and returned to the moment at hand.

"How do you ever leave here?" Samantha asked, aware of his presence but never taking her eyes from the surrounding mountains. "I'm afraid I'd sit on the porch and vegetate forever."

"I guess maybe I've gotten jaded. I go out that driveway at least once a day. Oh, a sunset catches my eye on occasion, or a particularly bright summer sky, but other than that it's all just...here. That must seem pretty strange to you?"

"Next to impossible, actually."

"Mind if I sketch you?" It had taken him a few minutes to work up the nerve to ask. "Standing like this, with that wondrous look on your face?"

She looked around at the bellowing, frolicking children. "I don't think Justin's quite that patient. Maybe later. When they settle down. How long would it take?"

Conrad put his hands on his hips. "Oh, that's right, we don't have much time, do we? Thanks for reminding me. You sure do know how to ruin a mood. Did you take lessons or come by it naturally?"

"Conrad, I didn't mean it that way. I..."

He stormed away, leaving her words hanging. He managed to rid himself of most of his anger before he got to the rest of the gang.

"Come on, Justin. Let's get those sleds out before all this stuff melts."

Conrad and Justin pulled large sheets of cardboard out of the barn. Rope handles looped through folded triple thicknesses of cardboard.

"How do you like our fancy sleds? I didn't have enough cardboard for everyone so we'll have to share. Think they'll work?" Conrad drew up even with Samantha, once again amazing her with his mood swings.

"Only one way to find out. Hop on Justin," she said as she took one of the handles from Conrad. Once they had made a wide loop around the bare oak tree, they pronounced it fit. Lisa sat Jessie on another piece and they all trudged through the deep snow to the treeless hill closest to the house. Kelsie hopped on about halfway to the top, hoping that Lisa wouldn't notice.

"Can't blame me for trying," she said when Lisa threw a handful of snow in her face.

"We're going to have to make some trails here before it gets slippery enough to really get moving down this hill," Conrad said. "Here, let me go first. I'm heavier and maybe my weight will pack it down a bit." Conrad made Justin get off as he climbed on. Balling his fists, he used them as ski poles to push himself off. He bogged down after about three feet. Try as he might, he couldn't budge that cardboard sled.

"Look out, Grampy. I bet I can do it." Justin waited for Conrad's go ahead before letting Kelsie push him off. His light body weight let him skim past Conrad and glide down the hill. "Come on, it's fun." he shouted up at them.

Lisa and Jessie went down next, grinning at Conrad who sat with a perplexed look on his face still only about a quarter of the way down the hill. Kelsie belly flopped on her sled and flew past him with a ridiculing sneer. Samantha waited at the top for someone to bring up one of the sleds. When they were too slow, she tried to push Conrad from his. He fought her off, trying in vain to get moving under his own power. They all gathered around, talking about him as if he weren't sitting right in front of them.

"Maybe if we put his feet behind him."

"Maybe we could lay him down on his belly, like I did."

"Maybe if we all pushed."

They gathered behind his back and began pushing on any part of him they could get their hands on. Samantha pulled on the rope from the front, and together they broke him free from the rut he had settled into. Samantha jumped on the board to keep from being run over. They moved slowly but steadily down the hill with Samantha's arms looped around Conrad's neck, trying to balance herself on the flimsy cardboard. Her feet flew out to the side and when it looked like they would both be thrown off, he pulled her to him, steadying the sled if not her heartbeat. By the time they reached the bottom, they were both laughing hysterically. Cheers drifted down from the crowd at the top.

"I don't remember sledding being this much fun, do you?" Conrad said softly as he nuzzled her ear.

"No. I certainly don't," she answered, pushing her cold face into the neckline of his jacket.

They all went up and down the hill so many times that even Justin lost count. By 11:00 hunger overtook them and they went inside, Justin protesting all the way. Samantha whipped up scrambled eggs with cheese and ham and called it brunch. They chattered endlessly about the snow fun they had been having and what they would do when they got back outside.

Conrad dampened the excitement when he mentioned naps, but everyone, especially the adults, needed the break. Conrad stretched out on the couch while Samantha tramped up the stairs to tuck the kids in. Then she fell across her bed and was instantly asleep. The girls sat in Lisa's room and gossiped quietly until they too fell asleep.

When the kids woke two hours later, they bundled up and put on the warm dry mittens that had been laid across the heat vents.

Lisa and Kelsie took the little ones up the hill to look for animal tracks. Conrad couldn't help but smile as he watched them obliterate any tracks within ten feet. He turned his attention to Samantha as soon as they crested the hill and disappeared.

She was standing twenty feet away in a fresh patch of snow, seemingly looking for something; turning around, craning her neck to check out the ground behind her. Then, without a word, she fell straight back, her arms and legs scissoring in the snow. Conrad walked over and stood at her feet, worrying that she might be having some kind of a weird seizure or something. Relieved to see the perfect snow angel she had made, he moved over and let his body fall a few feet from hers. Where she had scissored her legs and turned her angel into a girl, Conrad only moved his a little, forming pantlegs in the snow instead of a skirt. His boy snow angel joined hands with her girl one.

"Now who's going to help me up so I don't wreck my angel?" Samantha bellyached before turning to Conrad. Suddenly she was aware of the heat that filled his eyes, threatening to melt the snow beneath them. He rolled toward her and two pristine angels melded into one fat blimp angel as he lay half across the length of her body. His cold lips warmed against hers before he pulled away to look at her.

"I don't think angels do this kind of thing, do you?" Passion glazed her eyes and they crossed as she watched his lips lower again.

"Oh, I don't know. Feels pretty heavenly to me," Conrad whispered irreverently. He pulled his body fully on top of hers. Through the layers of jeans and insulated underwear, she could feel the need in his body and met it fervently with her own. His gloved hand was fighting its way through the many layers to her bra when he heard the whoops and hollers behind him. Pulling his hand away guiltily, he raised his head to watch her eyes cool. She reached her hands up and pulled his lips back to hers for one long, promising kiss, then rolled him off her before they could be clearly seen by the approaching kids.

"Grampy, I asked Lisy what you were doin and she told me you was making whoopie. Can you teach me how to make a whoopie?" Justin looked down at the two of them. "How come you're breathing funny?"

Conrad forced himself to glare at Lisa, then jumped up and grabbed Justin under the arms. He dragged him to a fresh patch of snow and laid him back into it.

"Okay, now pretend your flying. Legs too. That's it. Now give me your hand." Conrad pulled Justin up and showed him the angel he had made. Jessie came over beside them and looked with them at the form Justin had made in the snow.

"How come it don't look like yours? Yours has two heads. I want a two headed whoopie."

"It's not a whoopie, it's an angel and you have to be an adult to make two headed angels."

"Still looked like whoopie to me," Kelsie stage-whispered in Lisa ear and they collapsed into their own snickering angels on the ground.

Chapter 26

The rest of the day passed too quickly. After supper the kids played noisily in their bath, showing off for Lisa and Kelsie. Exhaustion shortened their "goodnights" and everyone went quietly to bed.

Samantha waited until the house was completely silent before she closeted herself in the bathroom and filled the claw-foot tub with hot water. She dropped a few Jello-soft balls of peach-scented bath oil into the water before climbing in and submerging everything from her chin down into the tranquilizing water, soothing her head to toe ache. Every muscle burned from the day-long abuse.

She tried not to splash around, but Conrad heard just the same. He wandered down the hallway, inhaling the delicate peach fumes coming from under the bathroom door. Had his house ever smelled this feminine? Julia had scoffed at womanly ways, unless it was in the bedroom, and then it was usually in someone else's. Lisa was still too young to really appreciate the joys of aroma therapy.

He sat cross-legged on the floor in front of the bathroom, listening to Samantha hum softly as she let the hot water work the kinks out of her body. When he heard her stand up and step out of the tub, every bone in his body wanted to open the door and join her. Instead, he made his way noiselessly back to his room. She probably wouldn't appreciate being spied on, even if this was his house.

He lay there contemplating all of the wonders she could bring into his life. She seemed so much more womanly and loving than

Julia ever had. Maybe she would even put lotion on her skin just for him, instead of before going out on the town. Better yet, maybe she would let him put the lotion on. Maybe even, somewhere down the road, they could share a peach-scented bath by candlelight. As he was falling asleep the distinctive aroma of Johnson's Baby Powder infiltrated the air of his room. He sighed contentedly, too close to sleep to dwell on how short-termed this arrangement was going to be.

Chapter 27

The next morning warmer temperatures and bright rays of sunshine had melted the snow enough to let it pack.

"Look, Grampy, I can make a ball now," Justin said the minute he jumped off the porch. He flung the odd shaped ball at Conrad's back.

Conrad smiled as he watched the snowball sail five feet from his side. "We need to work on your aim," he said without turning. When he did turn around it was to pitch a snowball straight at Justin's chest where it splattered, spraying his face with cold snow.

"That's not fair," Justin complained loudly. "You're bigger 'n me."

"Come on over here and we'll get in some target practice. Sam, would you help us?"

Samantha stood in the doorway of the house, listening to their conversation. Hesitantly she walked down the steps, keeping a close eye on the two of them.

"What exactly do you want me to do?"

"Just stand here," he said, positioning her body ten feet away from Justin. "This boy needs a little help with his aim and with that pretty red coat of yours, I figure you'd be a perfect target." Conrad moved her around until she was facing the house. Taking up a handful of snow, he drew a bulls-eye on the front of her coat. Then picked up more snow and packed it into a firm, compact ball.

"Hit me in the face and you're dead meat, Richmond. Got it?" Samantha tried to keep a stern look on her face.

Conrad grinned before he drew his arm back and chucked the ball at her, hitting her softly dead center in the stomach.

"See, it's that easy," he said bending over Justin.

Justin scooped up some snow and Conrad gave him tips on how to build a better snowball.

The first twenty or so missed her completely. Finally, with a lot of coaching from Conrad and egging on from Samantha, he was able to land a snowball on her hip. They both jumped up and down hugging him wildly at his success.

"Let's go see what those girls are up to," Conrad said shaking the cramp out his arm.

Samantha brushed off her coat and followed them to the other side of the house where a snowman was beginning to take shape.

Lisa and Jessie were making the middle ball, pushing it across the virgin snow. When they picked it up to set it on the bottom one, it crumbled in their hands.

Crocodile tears came into Jessie's eyes.

"Hey, kiddo," Kelsie said behind her. "If your Grampy catches you crying, he'll make you go in. Can't have your face freezing, he'll say. Come on, let's try again. I'll bet this time it'll work better."

Jessie smiled shyly up at Kelsie who was packing a large snowball in her hands. The girls all worked together at making this snowball grow, packing it down as they went. Soon they were all on their knees pushing the large ball through the deep snow.

Samantha and the boys built their own snowman and soon it was as bigger than the girls'.

"Ha ha. Ours is bigger," Justin crowed.

"That's cause our's is a lady," Jessie said as they realized the middle ball was indeed bigger than the bottom one.

"You're right, Jess. That's definitely a snowlady," Conrad said as he examined the buxom figure before him. "Why don't you guys go find stuff to make her look female and we'll go find stuff to make ours look male."

When they had finished gathering and applying sticks, stones, carrots and trimmings, they all stood back to admire their handiwork. The snow couple faced each other and the living room window where they could be appreciated from the warmth of the house.

"Whew! It's a ways up here, isn't it?" Samantha's words were more of a statement than a question. Sweat ran from the base of her neck and down between her shoulder blades, chilling her back in the freezing air. She could see the log structure above her, but it still seemed to be miles away.

"It doesn't seem that far when there isn't all this snow underfoot. By the time I get to the top, I've walked off most of my day's frustrations and headaches."

Samantha turned around and looked down the mountainside they had just climbed. Through the bare tree tops she could see the house. Smoke puffed steadily out of the main chimney and she could see the light over the kitchen table where Kelsie and Lisa sat with stacks of cookbooks, figuring out their surprise dinner menu. The smaller kids were taking late afternoon naps, exhausted from playing in the deep snow. Tied to the oak tree, two wood-plank swings blew in the soft wind. The snowman they had made this morning stood waving at the window on the front of the house. He stood erect and proud, not the crumbling mass he would soon become if the weather forecast was correct. Close beside him stood the definitely female snow person, a pinecone necklace decorating her more than ample bosom. A big red holiday bow was painfully staked in the top of her head. Beyond them and the house more mountains rose in the distance, gently mounded heaps of worn rock and trees. Snow brushed the tree limbs and bare black branches were highlighted against the glare of the white ground.

"It looks so homey and peaceful." There was a dreamy tone in Samantha's voice and she turned her head to see if Conrad was close enough to hear.

He was standing so near to her that her lips almost brushed his coat.

"Sorry," he said, backing up a half pace, though his eyes stayed glued to hers.

"Come on," Samantha said, quickly escaping the immediate peril of his lingering look by heading up the trail. "Show me where you do all your wonderful work, hillbilly."

"Hillbilly? Them's fightin' words in these parts. Get ready to get your face washed, Yankee." He ran at her and chased her the rest of the way to the studio, screaming and hollering all the way.

The porch was cleared of snow and smoke rose from this chimney. Conrad had snuck off earlier and lit a fire to warm the place so Samantha wouldn't be in a hurry to leave. He hoped.

They sat on the steps to catch their breath before going in. A squirrel chattered at them from a nearby branch, apparently angry at being woken up by all of the racket.

"Sorry, Chucky," Conrad called up to him. He walked over to a scarred wooden bin, raised the lid and pulled out a handful of acorns. Brushing the snow off the porch railing, he laid them on the edge nearest the complaining critter. "Here. Peace, little buddy?" From another bin he filled his hand with sunflower seeds. Then he sat back down beside Samantha on the step. "Shhhh. He'll come get them."

They watched as Chucky eyed Samantha cautiously. He obviously knew Conrad was no threat, but he found this new human to be loud and obnoxious. Finally hunger or greed convinced him to jump from his perch onto the roof of the porch. He ran head first down the porch post and grabbed a nut. Keeping an eye on them, he ran back the way he came and deposited it in the "Y" of his tree trunk before scurrying back for more. When the railing was clear, Conrad made a chattering noise and Chucky warily crossed the porch to Conrad's outstretched hand. He pulled the hand back slowly until Chucky was sitting on the step beside them, still eyeing Samantha. She watched as Conrad finger-fed his hungry little friend. When the seeds were gone, Conrad spoke softly.

"Are we friends again?" Chucky looked at him, then at Samantha, then ran back to his branch, chattering loudly all the way. Sitting near his nest, he watched them enter the cabin.

"I suppose you're going to try to make me believe you get a lot done up here," Samantha said as they crossed the threshold. "What with your little friend and all".

As Conrad closed the door behind them, Samantha looked around. A picture window filled one whole side of the room, displaying the mountains beyond in a huge wooden frame. Bright sunshine poured in and shone on a work table. A piece of fresh paper was secured there, waiting for his brush to bring it to life. Small pencil sketches of a sagging cantilevered barn edged by flowering bushes were clipped to the edge. Hand-printed notes on ideas, color and texture covered the rest of the page.

No curtains blocked a bit of the sunlight. A low fire burned in the pot-bellied stove, warming the room to bearable. Some of Conrad's paintings hung on the walls. Three stacks leaned up against the far wall.

Conrad tapped her shoulder and handed her a cup of coffee from the thermos he had brought.

"Thanks," she said, sipping the hot brew as she made her way around the studio. "You really are good, aren't you? I thought you were, but...I guess I was a little spellbound by the time you finished that one in town."

"I'm getting better," Conrad said modestly, glad she had admitted what he was afraid to voice. "Last month they hung one of my paintings in the art museum up in Knoxville. They said they liked the way it showed how things looked before we got discovered."

"Mind if I look?" Samantha asked before she started flipping through the leaning stack of paintings.

"No, go ahead." Conrad watched her expressions as she went through the pictures. This was part of the reason he brought her up here; to share with her the joy and the sadness he had gone through in the past few years.

She commented about the paintings, stopping at each one. The beauty and simplicity in these mountain scenes seeped out of every painting. Some were of places she recognized; houses in the cove, the rocks at Chimney Picnic Area. But most she had never seen; houses with wild roses growing up past broken windows, fields of purple iris clumps, an archaic wooden pump disintegrating from years of summer sunshine, spring rains and winter's ice. She considered asking if these were real places or only in his mind. Before she could put her thoughts into words, the pictures changed.

Conrad stood close behind her, looking over her shoulder. His breathing became more shallow as she came to the back of the stack.

She took one out and carried it over to the window to get a better look. Dreary rain filled the paper. Sighted from the living room window of his house, the yard was filled with mud, the barns gray and somber. A broken swing hung from a tree, its wooden plank cracked down the middle. Yet, in the distance, near the edge of the woods, a tiny redbud tree bloomed profusely through the drenching rain, its purple-pink blossoms adding the only dabs of color in the somber scene. She turned it over and read the date, April 8, 1989. Her eyes raised, questioning Conrad.

"I did that one a few days after Julia left. Abby was still home then but planning her wedding to Jim. Lisa was just starting to go through puberty. It was a real dark time for all of us. Even after all of the fighting and yelling, to have her walk away was devastating for the girls."

"And for you."

"Yeah, well, what can I say? Back then I felt like it was all my fault. Like I didn't try hard enough. Like I should have fought to keep her here. I felt that if I had been..."

"Been what? More loving, more forceful, more in control. What, Conrad? What could you have done that would have made her stay? And did you really want her to?"

"Yes, at the time I did. For the girls' sake, not my own. I never could figure how she could pick up and leave them. Me yes.

Heck, there's been times I'd like to leave me. But not them."
Conrad wore a puzzled look on his face even after all these years.
He shook it off, and tried to smile as he added, "Water under the
bridge, darlin'. Anyway, dark as those days were, there was always
an aura of hope. Someday life would get better."

He took the painting out her hand and she followed him back
to the stack. There was more he needed her to see. Much more.

Gradually the paintings got brighter. There was one of Abby
and Lisa with a vague reflection of Jim smiling brightly behind
Abby's right shoulder. Samantha recognized them from the
paintings in the Smoky Junction Restaurant and around the house.
Following that were paintings of babies in buggies, a teenage girl
with new-found rebellion in her stance, a very pregnant woman and
on to two small children teeter-tottering in summer sunshine.

Then suddenly, but not unexpectedly, the paintings went from
glowing color and happiness to pitch black and bitterness. The next
seven or eight paintings were filled with complete despair, different
from the ones of '89. No flecks of brightness sparkled anywhere
here. Ash gray and blood red filled the painting all the way to the
black-streaked edges. Enraged slashes criss-crossed from corner to
corner. Samantha didn't need to look for dates on these. She knew
when they had started.

"Why hang on to these?" she asked, not looking at Conrad.
"Why not throw them away instead of keeping all of this pain
locked up in here."

"Don't you see? I have to keep them. They keep me on an
even keel and show the only time in my life when I truly lost faith.
In myself, in my God, in life itself. They are a reminder that even
when things get out of hand, they aren't this bad. Understand?"
Please, his eyes begged.

"Yes." She did understand. Even if…back up…when she left,
it couldn't hurt him as bad as Abby's death did. Nothing would
ever hurt him that bad again, unless he lost Lisa or one of his
grandchildren. She knew she would feel the same way if anything
ever happened to Kelsie, Jeff or the baby growing inside Carrie. A

deep shudder ran through her and she put the paintings down in their slots before she turned to pull Conrad into her arms.

They held each other tightly, showing feelings of compassion instead of passion. Darkness shrouded the path as they headed down the mountain an hour later.

Chapter 28

Conrad hooked the old horse up to the older sleigh. It had been out in the back yard ever since Conrad could remember. Much worn, the red paint had all but vanished from the surface, leaving a softened pinkish-gray hue to the battered wood. Good background for a print, he thought absentmindedly as he rattled it a few times to make sure it was solid enough to haul them. Jessie and Justin chased each other around in the snow, snaking their way through the trees and bushes. Conrad had hollered at them earlier when they kept getting too close to Petal's feathery feet.

Petal was a huge Belgian mare, belying the delicate name Lisa had given her ten years ago when she was little more than a yearling. Through the years they had made sure she was well exercised, but this past year had slid by without much more than food and a little love for the gentle giant. Conrad knew he'd have to keep a close eye on her on the way to and from Ada's place.

Samantha eyed the back hips that were well above her head. "Will she be okay?" she asked quietly, walking up to Conrad's side while he adjusted the harness.

"I think so. We'll take it slow. Besides, it's only about a mile down the road and the snow will make the pulling easy. She looks happy enough about the whole thing, don't you think?"

If horses could smile, Samantha thought this one probably was. Maybe it was being out with the family again and the attention she was getting, but Petal seemed content with the idea and ready to get started.

"Here, I'll take those blankets now. Climb on and I'll hand the kids up to you."

Conrad made a stirrup of his hands and boosted her up into the front seat, watching her ascent and the tightness of her bluejeans as her backside wobbled in front of his eyes. He handed her threadbare woolen blankets which she lay across the splintered seats.

Much to the little ones' dismay, Conrad insisted on Lisa and Kelsie sitting on the outside edges. They compromised by sliding closer to the middle and letting Justin and Jessie sit on their laps.

Samantha helped Conrad tuck blankets around them. The evening was clear, but cold seeped through their heavy clothes. She sat close to Conrad on the front seat, tucking her arm under his elbow and enjoying the warmth of his body. He let the back of his arm rest against the curve of her breast, even though it did crazy things to him. Resting one hand on Samantha's leg, he let Petal set her own docile pace as she pulled the sleigh through the soft drifts of snow. The bells he had threaded through her harness jingled merrily every time she took a step. Samantha closed her eyes and enjoyed the perfect moment. Conrad moved his hand off her leg and put his arm around the back of the seat, pulling her into the pit of his arm as he did. She snuggled in, happy to be near him and the warmth of his goose down jacket. When he put his lips to her forehead, she looked up into his eyes. She put her hand on the back of his neck and pulled his head down until his lips met hers.

Justin gave the kiss time to get mushy before he piped up from the seat directly behind them. "Ohhhh, Grampy. I saw that. I'm gonna tell."

Conrad ever so slowly tore his lips from the overwhelming magical pull Samantha had on them. He looked back over his shoulder at four foolishly grinning kids.

"First of all, exactly who are you going to tell?"

Justin was stumped by that one, but not for long. "Mrs. Pillars, that's who. She might spank you or make you go to bed without supper."

Conrad looked down at Samantha's face. "Hmmmm," he said so low no one else heard.

Justin coughed loudly when he saw his grampa getting all goofy-eyed again.

"Second of all," Conrad resumed, "you're too young to know this but sleighs were made for smooching and hugging."

"Yuk, Grampy, you're sick. Hey, Kelsie, give me a kiss, Grampy says it's okay." Kelsie reached over and gave him a loud, wet kiss right on the lips. Before long, everyone on the seat was kissing, hugging and laughing joyfully at their silliness.

Conrad kissed Samantha fleetingly before he snapped the reins. "Come on, Petal, time's a wastin'."

Ada was ready to go when they reached her house. Carl was snowed in up in Knoxville and she missed the comfort of his company, even to the extent of turning the TV on to ESPN so she could pretend he was there. She had been relieved when Conrad had called with his invitation, partially because she was bored and partially because she was curious about this woman beside him now on the sleigh. They had talked briefly on the phone, and Ada had tried to make Samantha feel welcome.

Conrad jumped down and helped her up beside Samantha on the front seat. She put her overnight bag between her knees and cheerfully greeted the bundled forms behind her as she sat down. Conrad introduced her to Samantha who was absorbed by the friendliness in the older lady's face. She laid a mittened hand on Samantha's gloved ones.

"I'm so glad to finally be able to put a face with the voice on the phone. I taught Conrad not to lie and he wasn't when he said you were a right pretty little thing."

Samantha had a hard time accepting the compliment from the country-beautiful woman beside her. Her beauty wasn't store-bought but came from within. An inner peace radiated through every wrinkle of her well-lined face.

"I've heard so much about you," Samantha said as she leaned forward to see around Conrad's chest. "I feel like I know you from all the stories the kids and Conrad have told me."

"Not the ugly ones, I hope. Justin, you didn't tell her about the time I told you that gummy worms were real worms with sugar on them, did you? They each had a brown sugar coated worm in their mouths before I could get to them." Her laughter perked up Petal's ears.

"Were you singing "Jingle Bells" on the way over here?" Ada asked, as Conrad guided Petal through a wide U-turn in the road.

"Yeah," Justin blabbed, "but we were busy doing other fun things too. You shoulda seen us. We was smooching and carrying on just like Grampy and Sammy. Grampy started it. He said that's what sleighs are for. For kissing and stuff. Pretty yukky, if you ask me."

"Nobody asked you, boy." Conrad and Samantha kept their eyes on the road ahead as Ada glanced from one to the other. Her eyes rested on Conrad until he finally had to look at her. She kept her face straight for a few seconds, then let the smile creep from her eyes to her cheeks and mouth.

"Well, I'll be," she said to no one in particular. No one in particular had any further comments.

Chapter 29

"Supper's almost ready," Conrad announced when they entered the house. "Why don't you women folk sit here in the living room while we get it on the table?"

Kelsie and Lisa promptly plopped down on the couch, watching Conrad's expression.

"Nice try, girls. Now get your bony bottoms out in that kitchen and set the table."

The two women sat companionably, neither one needing to say a word. Sounds of glasses rattling and dishes clinking rang out from the kitchen. Ada pulled on her hand-knitted slippers and crossed her ankles on the footstool.

"Did Conrad tell you how long we've been together?"

"He said that when he was growing up there wasn't much of anybody around to love him, except you and Carl."

"Yep, his father lit out when he was three. Probably the kindest thing he ever did for the boy. He was a no-account if ever there was one. His mother turned into a full-time drunk after that. Poor thing. She really tried to stay sober for his sake, but she kept falling off the wagon. Finally killed her. Indirectly, that is. She got drunk over in Ashville one night. The man she was shacking up with pulled a knife on her. She fought dying for three days before finally giving up."

"Conrad told me she died when he was young but he didn't say how."

"He was fourteen at the time and insisted I take him over there to see her in the hospital. She never came to while he was there. Never got to tell him that she really did love him, or hear those words back from him. He stayed by her side 'til well after she'd grown cold. Like to broke my heart to watch him."

"He says you've saved him more than once. That you became mother and best friend to him. Said Carl was the father he never had."

"I love that boy as much as if he was my own and I love him every bit as much now that he's a man." Her eyes began flashing angrily as she talked. "That no good Julia just about ruined him. First she dragged him to Nashville. Said she was unhappy here. Bored. He moved up there to please her. That's where Abby and Lisa were born. He hated it up there for seven long years. He'd come back for a visit and his eyes would be sunken and he'd look so miserable."

"Seven years can seem like a hundred when you're unhappy," Samantha said, speaking of her own past as well as Conrad's.

"Well, finally, about the time his paintings started to become popular, he convinced her he'd make more money around here. That was important to her, so they moved back into this house. I soon found out she was sleeping around, she'd tell you it was to ease the boredom caused by living with Conrad.

Samantha thought about all the fun she'd had in Conrad's presence these past few days. How could anyone say he was boring? Tantalizing maybe. Perplexing, frustrating, and maybe a little bit overwhelming. But boring? Never.

"I knew about it," Ada continued. "I figured deep down, he did too. It about crushed him when she left. Out of the blue, she comes home with this blond haired, blue eyed kid. Couldn't a been much more than twenty five, twenty eight tops. As a matter of fact, I could tell Abby was wondering if she should flirt with him, thought maybe Mom had brought him home for her. Julia waltzes up to Conrad...we were all in the kitchen fixing supper...and says, 'This is Paul. We're taking the next flight for L.A.. I'll file for divorce out there.' She threw only her best clothes and jewelry in a suitcase while we all stood in the kitchen and stared at Paul. He was a looker, all right, but he didn't even have the gumption to meet our eyes. Stood there, leaning against that old kitchen sink and stared at his feet the whole time Julia was packing. Then she pranced back through the kitchen, kissed Conrad on the cheek, told the girls to be good, took that boy's hand and waltzed out the door."

"She didn't even hug or kiss the girls goodbye? Never said she'd send for them or anything?"

"Nope. 'Be good', that was all. I guess she thought that was about enough motherly advice. Even when she called later, she only wanted to talk to Conrad. Then it was "send me this, pay me that, I want, I want, I want.""

Conrad stood with his ear against the door, eavesdropping as Ada spilled his life story. He had figured she would, but was uncertain why he had set her up for it.

"Dad!" Lisa stood indignantly behind him, hands on her hips. "You tell us never to do that, but there you are, pressed up to that door listening to their private conversation. We need to have a nice long talk about practicing what you preach, old man."

A sheepish expression crossed his face. Lisa moved up and stood close to him. "What are they saying?"

"I hear voices behind that door," Ada said, lowering her voice to a murmur.

They sat in silence, listening to the lack of noises from the kitchen. Grinning slyly, they took up the conversation again.

"Yes, Conrad pretty much fell apart after that. For the most part he was a good dad. He had pretty much raised those girls anyway, what with Julia gallivanting all over the county and beyond. He listened to their fears, cuddled them when they cried, tried to get them to see that there was a bright side to life.

"But I'll never forget what happened about a year after Julia moved away. He started drinking real heavy, going out to the bars 'til all hours of the night, coming home smelling like Jack Daniel's and cheap perfume."

"He did? Sweet, innocent Conrad?"

"Sure enough. One night he brought these floozies home, two of 'em. I tried to stop him at the door but he weaved them right past me. Started kissing on both of them right in front of the girls. I tell you, it was disgusting! He had one half naked before..."

"What are you telling her? Honest to God, Samantha, it's not true! I never..." Conrad was through the door before he realized he'd been had. Slapping his hand to his forehead, he hurried back into the kitchen.

In the living room the two women laughed themselves to tears, hand in hand as they tried, in vain, to regain control of themselves.

"Conrad wants me to tell you that if you're finished making fun of him, it's time to eat." Kelsie held the door for them, wondering what she had missed.

Conrad kept his back to them as he stood at the stove dishing up the chili.

"Smells good," Samantha said as she came up behind him. She laid her hand on the small of his back, reached up to kiss his reddened neck, then sidled around until she could see his face. It still had an almost scalded look as he glared into the pot. His jaw was tight and the muscles in his neck stood out like cords.

"You deserved that, and you know it," she whispered. "But I'm glad she told me all that she did. It explains a lot."

He looked away from the bubbling kettle and into her eyes. "I'm glad too. Especially the part about the half naked women. I didn't know how I was going to tell you about them."

"Hey, when you two get done making goo-goo eyes over there, we'd like to eat some time tonight."

Conrad ladled out bowls of chili for the small kids, then dumped a little more "Joe's Hell Sauce" into the pan and carried it over to the table. He'd teach them to make fun of him.

Chapter 30

Through the meal everyone kept the conversation light and cheery. They all had extra portions of milk, questioning Conrad about the chili being hotter than normal. He simply grinned in response. By the time they had finished Ada's blackberry cobbler, the little ones' eyes had begun to droop. Lisa and Kelsie graciously excused themselves and carried the sniffling children to bed.

The three of them sat around the table, drinking decaf coffee and talking about the weather and every insignificant thing that came into their heads.

Conrad nudged Ada's foot with his own. She looked at him questioningly, then understood the sturdy cue he was giving her.

"How long were you married, Samantha?" she asked, supposedly out of the blue.

"Twenty-two years."

"It must have been a good marriage for it to last that long. What changed? If you don't mind my asking."

"Nothing changed, except to go from bad to worse. It took me a long time to wise up to the fact that things were never going to get any better. Slow learner, I guess. I'll never forget the feeling I had when I realized that we would grow old and life would still be the same. Two bickering old fools who may have loved each other once, but never did seem to like each other much. Can you understand that?" She was looking at Conrad now.

He nodded, not wanting to say a word for fear of breaking the flow of her words.

"We reached a point where we didn't fight anymore, that took too much energy. I guess you might say we sniped at each other. He made me feel worthless, and I made him feel...Oh, hell, I never did know how I made him feel.

"Finally things started to really go down hill. We would be having a conversation, both of us still trying to get along. Trying to decide how we were supposed to act and react. All of a sudden, I'd say one word, the wrong one I guess, I never did figure out what it was. He would erupt like Mount Vesuvius, seemingly burning through my mind and leaving trails of pain as molten hot as lava."

She took a deep breath and sighed heavily, as if the weight of the consequences was too heavy for her to bear. "We started out wrong, stayed wrong and ended wrong. Finally, I had to get out. Jeff was on his own by then and he was glad I got out. But I don't think Kelsie's forgiven me for it yet." She looked pensively towards the door that Kelsie had recently gone through.

Conrad listened silently, wanting to touch her, hold her, comfort her, assure her he'd never be like that, but wanting even more to hear the rest of her story. He forced himself to remain still and simply listen.

She looked around as if she'd been only thinking these things. Knowing that she had poured out so much of her private self made her squirm in her seat. She never talked about the bad times of her marriage to anyone. Never.

"Anyway, I filed for divorce and that was that."

She escaped to stand at the window over the sink. Conrad started to follow, but Ada put out a restraining hand.

The half moon reflected serenely over the snow man and woman they had made that afternoon. The kids had insisted on making them lovebirds, their branch arms intertwining, their black stone mouths smiling only for each other. Tomorrow, if Justin has his way, a "til melt do us part" wedding would take place.

The neighboring mountains were clearly visible in the pale moonlight. She pulled herself together, forcing herself to ignore the leverage she had given these people. They knew her weaknesses now and she prayed they wouldn't use them against her.

She returned to the table, giving both of them a shy smile. Conrad stood without a word and walked over to the window, leaned against the sink and looked out at the dark sky. Crossing back to Samantha, he put his hands on the back of her chair.

"Ada, do you mind if Samantha and I go outside for a minute? There's something I want to show her."

"No, no of course not. You kids go ahead. I need to talk to Lisa about some 4-H business anyway."

Once they had bundled up in their coats, scarfs, and boots it didn't seem too cold. They stood on the porch letting their eyes adjust to the dim light. Conrad took Samantha's hand and led her down the stairs. In the distant barn Petal whinnied.

"Night, old girl," Conrad called across the yard.

He led Samantha towards the row of pine trees. Her heart raced at the warmth flowing from Conrad's gloves. When they reached the middle of the pines, right where the earth started to gently lift towards the high summit of the mountain behind the house, Conrad lay down on his back and waited patiently for Samantha to join him.

She hesitated a long moment. "Here? Now?" her eyes asked but he was looking up at the sky, not at her.

When she finally lowered herself to the ground, she was a good foot and a half from him. After sitting tensely for a few seconds she relaxed enough to look for what had drawn Conrad's attention. Above the pine boughs that wreathed the view, the winter sky was full of stars. She lay back to enjoy the full effect. Out here the lights from the city were but a vague memory. The moon was low in the sky and behind the trees. The stars shone as bright specks of light in a midnight blue background.

"Oh Conrad," Samantha whispered.

"I've tried so hard to capture this," Conrad said, taking hold of her hand. "You saw my attempts in the studio. I can't seem to come even close no matter how many times I try. But it seems I keep right on working at it anyway."

"The stars seem so much brighter here. Must be the big city lights blot them all out at home."

"Yeah, that and we're closer to them."

"Sure, Conrad. Like a few hundred feet higher is going to make a difference when you're talking millions of miles."

She stopped talking as his arresting smile caught her off guard. Scootching across the chilly snow until her hip rested against his, she lay like a Puritan mummy beside him. He released her hand and wrapped his arm beneath her neck. She took his hand at her shoulder and held it tightly, her head resting against the side of his chest.

"Samantha?" Conrad waited for her to look up at him before continuing. "You know I'd never treat you like he did, don't you?"

"Yes, I know."

"Okay." That was all either of them needed to say about the matter and the subject was closed, for now.

They relaxed in each other's arms, watching the stars dance in the sky. Both saw the shooting star at the same time and both made their own silent wishes, hand tightening in hand, passing the wishes from one to the other.

"Starlight, starbright, first star I see tonight, I wish I may, I wish I might, have the wish I wish tonight." Samantha said it softly and slowly. They both wished for this closeness never to end. Tomorrow was in the future and they both vowed not to let it invade the here and now of this night.

After many minutes of peaceful contentment, Samantha spoke dreamily. "Conrad?"

"Hmmmmm?"

"My butt's freezing to the ground."

"Mine too. I suppose we ought to go in before they find us frozen like this in the morning." He pulled himself up and leaned over her, waiting for her eyes to ask for his kiss. When they did, he rested his lips on hers.

The kiss became a measure of the feelings that were growing so strong between them, no matter what their daytime voices said. Honest and sweet turned to long and lustful. The fantasy world of this night was their reality and no matter what they said or did to each other during the coming days, tonight's truth wouldn't be denied.

After what seemed like hours, good sense took over. There were worse positions that the kids could find them frozen into in the morning. Standing up and adjusting their clothes, they made their way to the house, neither satisfied nor unsatisfied.

Chapter 31

Sunday morning dawned bright and not nearly as cold. The snow was melting and they all knew their days together were numbered. Everyone except Justin and Jessie. They were still young and foolish enough to have faith in the new happiness they had found.

Conrad stood at the stove fixing pancakes while Samantha fried bacon at his side. The kids had worked together to set the table and now were sitting together, talking and laughing. Ada sat beside the table with her knitting. She was enjoying being waited on for a change and watched the scene around her with matriarchal pride.

"I think we can get to church if we put the van in four-wheel drive," Conrad said to Lisa as she poured orange juice into mismatched glasses. "Would you like to go with us, Sam? Kelsie?"

"Oh, Conrad, we didn't bring anything to wear," she answered, mentally checking through the clothes she had hung in the guest room closet while frantically searching for excuses not to go. "Just our jeans and sweats. Sorry, but I'll stay here and start dinner. That beef roast will take a while to cook."

"Nobody's going to care what you're wearing," Ada said gently. "Everyone will be so glad to be able to get out, I'll bet no one will even notice you're there. And I'll put the roast in the oven while you get ready."

"You can go through my stuff and pick out something," Lisa volunteered. "I've got lots of sweaters and stirrup pants."

Samantha looked over at Lisa who was a good five inches taller than she was. "Yeah, right."

"Well, at least the sweaters should fit," Lisa said answering her questioning look. "And we just washed all of your jeans so they'll be fine. Please come with us. I want Kelsie to meet some more of my friends."

"Please, Mom."

"Please, Sammy."

"Yeah, Sammy, please."

"It would be nice, Samantha."

Conrad smiled over the top of her head at the kids. What a team all they made.

"OK, OK. I'll go. Let's eat quick so we'll have time to get dressed. But I've got to find something other than jeans."

Seeing Conrad in a suit was almost more than Samantha could handle. The dark navy wool pulled the blue out of his eyes. She watched him adjust his tie in the mirror over the buffet. He hadn't seen her yet and she wondered if he would comment one way or the other on her dress.

He caught the reflection of her watching him and his heart skipped more than one beat as he gazed at her over his shoulder. Turning around slowly, he gave a low, slow wolf whistle, and was surprised that he actually remembered how.

"Wow!"

"Thanks. You look pretty darned handsome yourself."

"Is that Lisa's? I mean, I don't remember seeing it before."

"I think it's a mini dress on her, but on me I think it's respectable." She glanced doubtfully down the burgundy print dress to her nyloned knees. "Don't you?"

"It looks great. Trust me."

She stood in front of him and straightened his collar, her fingers on his neck nearly driving him crazy. He forced himself to remain still while tainted thoughts raced through his mind.

"Ready, Grampy? Sammy? The van's all brushed off and Lisa got it turned around in the driveway. She didn't even get stuck. Let's go."

Conrad helped Samantha with her jacket then motioned for her to take the lead, enjoying the view as he followed.

As they pulled into the parking lot of the small country church, Justin finger-counted the cars. A bell pealed from the small steeple as people made their way to the door, cautious of the icy parking lot. Everyone wore smiles and gabbed like long lost relatives.

"Hey, Conrad, how do ya like this weather?" an older man hollered out across the lot when Conrad stepped out of the car.

"Fine, Joe. Makes me feel like one of them crazy Northern-ers."

Samantha hesitated as she opened her car door. Maybe this wasn't such a good idea afterall. Conrad came around and took her hand.

"Crazy, huh?"

"Oh come on, Darlin'. Everybody's friendly. Nobody's going to bite, I promise." He pulled her to her feet.

"Grampy, will you carry me? I'll get my pretty shoes all icky if you don't." Jessie held up her arms at the rear door.

"Sure, Honey." Gracefully Conrad reached in and picked her up, making a seat out of his arm for her.

Justin climbed out and reached for Samantha's hand.

"Come on, Sammy, let me help you. Careful now, it's real slippery over here." Justin gripped her hand in his and guided her to the door and up the steps.

Lisa and Kelsie walked with Ada between them, chatting with a couple of Lisa's friends.

"I figured you'd be here," a deep voice said from behind them. They all turned to see Carl coming towards them across the parking lot. Ada's face lit up as he kissed her soundly on the lips. "Missed you, old girl."

Ada slapped playfully at the front of his coat. "Me too, you old codger." She linked her arm through his and they made their way to the church.

The urge to have this kind of happiness flooded over both Samantha and Conrad. Could they really find this kind of love and commitment?

The minute they were through the door, Conrad grabbed Samantha's hand in his free one. There would be no mistaking his intent now and it was too late to pull her hand away and make a run for it without causing a scene. She looked up into his eyes and even though she felt everyone watching, she had to smile.

Though it wasn't as friendly as he would have liked, Conrad figured any smile was better than none. He made his way through the old church. Of course he had to stop and say a few words to everyone they passed. But he made it a point not to introduce her, playfully enjoying the eager curiosity in their faces. At the end of the third pew from the front Conrad pulled her aside, letting Lisa and Kelsie go in first.

"I'll sit between Kelsie and Sammy. Okay Grampy?" Justin asked tugging Samantha's hand, not waiting for an answer.

Conrad let go of her other hand, then followed her into the pew. When they sat down, Jessie squirmed out of Conrad's arms and reached for Samantha.

Hazy memories of clean damp hair and bedtime stories assailed her senses as Jessie nestled into her lap. She looked up at the statue of Jesus hanging on the wall of the church and said a silent prayer for strength.

Conrad leaned over to whisper in her ear. "That's Bernie over there in the second row. The one who was working at the Bon Air the other night. Did you ever introduce yourself to him?"

Samantha blushed, embarrassed by his veiled reference to the night they had embraced in front of her motel room.

"And that's Pastor Hulbert. Don't be surprised if he makes over you and wants me to introduce you to everyone. He'll probably make you stand up in front of God and everybody. Literally." Conrad was grinning.

Frightened, she rose up from her seat, ready to flee no matter what the cost. Just then the piano began to play the opening for "The Church in the Wildwood." Everyone stood up around her and began to sing.

Harmonious voices filled the church to the rafters as Samantha resigned herself to see this through. She let her eyes wander to the faces of the people around her. Some seemed to leer but most shyly smiled. Ada waved at them from across the aisle. Carl sat beside her. Samantha would have to ask later how he had made it back from Knoxville already. She raised her hand slightly and waved back.

Turning, she gazed at Conrad whose deep voice rose confidently in song. This man beside her was truly something else. She linked her arm through his and let her slightly off key soprano voice join in.

"Let us pray." Pastor Hulbert intoned from the pulpit. "Heavenly Father, we thank you for allowing us the privilege to come to your house today to worship you. Thank you for clearing the snow from the roads so we could get through."

Samantha followed the prayer closely, her eyes open only enough to keep her body from swaying. Yet she was still caught unaware when the Pastor thanked God for the visitors who were joining them today. She glanced around the church, hoping against hope to find other people who looked as out of place as she felt.
"Conrad and his bunch have had it real rough this past year. We hope you'll do everything in your power to make the future brighter for them. They're good folks, God. Why, Conrad's been working day and night on them paintings of his to try and make a life better for Lisa and Abby 'n Jim's kids."

"Is this an infommercial?" she sacrilegiously whispered into Conrad's ear. He smiled slightly, pretending to ignore her.

"Please, God, let these new rays of sunshine stay at their door to brighten their lives."

"Amen," someone said across the room. Was that Ada or was somebody else in on this too?

"We ask these things in the name of the Father, the Son and the Holy Spirit. Amen and amen."

Conrad flexed the muscle in his arm, squeezing Samantha's hand as they sat down. Tears threatened to spill from her eyes and she missed most of the rest of the sermon, her mind reeling over the choices this man, his preacher and their God were asking her to make.

She rested her chin on Jessie's head. Jessie drew back and gazed up into her eyes. Her finger caught a tear as it spilled down Samantha's cheek and she sucked it off the salty fingertip.

As soon as the sermon had been said, the last hymn had been sung and Pastor Hulbert said, "Go in peace", the congregation flocked around them. Conrad tried to keep up with the introductions and Samantha tried to keep up with the names. Some of the men slapped Conrad on the back. A couple of the older women tenderly reached up and pinched his cheek as if he was a favorite little boy caught with his hand in the cookie jar.

"Conrad, Samantha, can y'all join us for supper Tuesday night," someone asked. The innocent question silenced the small group.

Conrad waited for Samantha's answer but she seemed unable to speak.

"We'll have to wait and see how the roads are, Bekka," Conrad answered for her. "If they're good enough, Samantha and Kelsie will have to head home before then. They've both got school to get back to, Samantha being a teacher and all."

"Hey, Pastor, can we say a quick prayer for a ton more snow?" someone from the back of the group shouted. "I think these two need a little more time together."

"Amen to that." Pastor Hulbert said as he took Samantha's arm from Conrad and walked her out the church door, talking quietly to her about something Conrad couldn't hear. As the bright sunlight assailed her eyes she handed Jessie to him. He was standing beside her and trying to hear what the Pastor was saying.

"You're welcome to come back any time," Pastor Hulbert continued. "Conrad, come see me in a few days, okay? There's something we need to discuss." He winked at Conrad as he turned his attention back to the crowd that stood behind him.

"I'm sorry," Conrad said softly as he opened the car door for her. He seemed to be saying that a lot lately.

"No you're not. Besides, these folks care about you and only want you to be happy. How lucky you are to have so many friends who love you. I'd give anything to have that kind of respect and affection."

"Would you, Samantha? Anything?"

"Nice try, Richmond. Let's head for home. Those look like snow clouds."

They all looked up at the darkening sky and laughed at the thought that the whole congregation was willing to deal with more snow just for the sake of their blooming feelings.

Conrad tried not to add meaning to the fact that Samantha had called his house "home". As if it belonged to her too.

Chapter 32

"Samantha?" Justin's whine came up the stairs, under the door and over to the bed where she was trying to read. After church they had dished up the huge Sunday dinner Ada had helped prepare. It was complete with beef roast, potatoes, assorted other vegetables and Lisa's favorite blueberry muffins. Samantha made green Jello and a pumpkin pie.

Ada had gone home with Carl, even though they all insisted both of them join them for dinner. She had gazed up into Carl's face and firmly said no. She was giggling like a schoolgirl when Carl helped her into his old pickup.

At dinner everyone ate too much, moaning as they left the table. The girls had taken off cross country skiing so it was just the four of them in the house. Jessie was napping and Justin was supposed to be. It was Conrad's turn to do the dishes and she could hear him half-singing, half-humming along with the kitchen radio.

When Justin was in one of his ornery moods, he added syllables to her name, stretching it out until it almost sounded like an obscenity. When he was his normal, happy self, she was simply Sammy.

Samantha stayed silent, hoping he would give up and go away. She had found that the only place she could get any peace in this house was closeted away in her room. Sometimes she needed that; to get away from the kids and from Conrad's none to subtle persistence.

"Samantha?" his voice was more insistent now and she knew he would continue until she answered him.

"What, Justin? I'm taking a nap."

Mumbles came up the stairway, too garbled to be understood.

"I can't hear you."

More mumbles.

She was across the room and had the door thrown open in seconds. "What?" she barked, glaring down at him from over the banister.

Justin face clouded over and he started to cry, repeating his words below the fists that rubbed at his eyes.

"I can't understand a single word you're saying. Speak up! And stop sniveling."

Conrad stood in the kitchen doorway, waiting to go to somebody's rescue, just as soon as he could figure out whose. Other than church this morning, they had been snowed in for three days, and tempers were starting to get a little short.

He knew better than anyone how Justin's whining could drive you nuts. But he couldn't let her make him cry like that. He dried his hands on the dish towel and went into the dining room. Standing at the bottom of the stairs, Justin heard him coming. He threw himself at Conrad's knees, wetting them with his tears and slobbers, then mumbled something about Samantha that Conrad couldn't make out.

Conrad looked up at Samantha standing on the landing, trying to keep rebuke from his eyes. He's just a little boy, he can't help it, he tried to silently tell her as he held Justin against his legs.

But she did see the censure in his eyes. After all the years of never being good enough, never acting the right way, never measuring up to David's standards, it was about the worst message he could have sent.

And he saw shades of Julia in her uglier days. On the days when she abused him and the children, verbally hinting that their closeness was somehow perverted.

"I'll take Justin in the kitchen with me." It was all he could safely say for the moment.

"Okay. I'm going to read for a bit, then take a nap." She closed the door quietly on the scene below.

Justin finally lay down on the couch with Conrad and they both napped. The anger in Julia's voice played over and over in Conrad's head. No, not Julia's. Samantha's. Was that a Freudian slip of the mind or what? Truthfully, there was little in Julia to compare with Samantha. Julia had never been the kind, sweet, loving person he already knew Sam to be. Right? She was kind, sweet and lovable, wasn't she? Just tired, that was all. Wasn't it?

"How come she yelled at me like that, Grampy?" was the first thing Justin asked when he started to fidget and woke Conrad up. "I was just askin' her to read me a story. That's all."

"I'm sorry, Justin. I shouldn't have hollered at you."

Neither one of them had heard Samantha come down and sit in the chair kitty-corner from the couch. She had obviously been there for a while, watching them both as they slept. Conrad unobtrusively wiped the corner of his mouth with the back of his hand, hoping he hadn't drooled.

"I was really tired, that's all. You gotta remember that I'm not used to little kids anymore. In my classroom we have a 'no whine' rule. And my own kids are all grown up. Well almost anyway," she added, remembering the temper tantrums Kelsie had thrown at Conrad a few days ago.

"S' okay, Sammie. I'm sorry I was whiny."

Jessie came into the room dragging the big rag doll Samantha had stitched up on the old treadle sewing machine the day before and carrying her coloring book and crayons. She sat down on the floor in front of the TV.

"Wanna color?" she asked Justin.

"Sure," he answered, extracting himself from the afghan. "Let's go to the table, though. The light's better in there." He gave Samantha a quick peck on the cheek as he raced by to beat Jessie to the table.

Conrad and Samantha sat not speaking for a while, listening to the happy ramblings from the dining room.

After a while Samantha spoke. "I remember now how it used to drive me crazy when Jeff and Kelsie would whine like that. But I gotta admit, I handled it a little better back then."

"It was so long before Justin started making any sound at all that I guess I forgot how annoying his voice can sound. Thank God, he doesn't do it very often."

"I'm sorry, Conrad. Sorry that I was so rude to your boy."

"And I'm sorry, too."

"You? For what?"

"For all the scary thoughts that went through my head about you."

A sardonic smirk crossed her lips. "Then I guess we're even."

******

Chapter 33

Listening to WDLY on the radio, they fixed sandwiches and soup. The weather man announced that tonight a warm rain should have most of the roads cleared and driving would be back to normal.

"Whatever that is," the disc jockey joked.

They all knew what that meant. Conrad and Samantha avoided each others eyes. Lisa and Kelsie sent knowing looks behind their backs. Justin and Jessie looked back and forth between the grown-ups wondering about all the long faces. By the time they sat down to eat, gloom hung over the table like a soggy cold blanket.

"You got your homework done, Lisa?" Conrad asked, more to break the silence than anything else. "I'll bet there'll be school tomorrow."

"No, but I only have History and I can finish that up tonight. There was supposed to be a test on the Civil war last Monday. Everything from Bull Run to Chickamauga. What a pain. I don't see why we have to know all this stuff. Do you, Kelsie?"

She looked up from her plate when Kelsie didn't answer. Her eyes followed the path from Kelsie's to Conrad and Samantha.

Conrad's hold on Samantha's hand was so tight that her fingers were turning white. Tears spilled freely down her cheeks, though certainly not from the pain of his grip.

They dropped back into silence, no one eating, all mesmerized by the almost visible pain that settled over the room.

Even Justin, for once, sat quietly watching. Finally, when it became unbearable to hold his tongue any longer, he broke the spell.

"Can we have ice cream now?"

Samantha sniffled, wiped her eyes with an unused corner of her napkin and forced a smile.

"I think ice cream is the best idea you've had all day. Chocolate or butter pecan?" she asked as she walked to the freezer.

"Silly. Chocolate of course," Justin giggled. "Butter pecan is for old folks. Like you."

"Justin Lee!" Conrad barked.

"Well, that's what Lisa told me. Didn't you?" He turned to Lisa to get him out of this last bit of trouble he had gotten himself into.

"I didn't say 'like Samantha'. I said old people like Butter Pecan ice cream, and since you like it, Justin put two and two together. Sorry."

"Not a problem, Lisa. I seem to recall your dad eating his share and then some. Hey Justin, does that mean he's old too?" She was grateful for the break in the tension, even if it was at her own expense.

"My Grampy ain't old."

Conrad smiled smugly at Justin and then at everyone else.

"Nope, he ain't old. He's ancient." Justin's timing was perfect, even for a six year old.

Laughter broke out around the table and suddenly everyone had a million things to say on this, their last night together.

"You'll be gone when we wake up, won't you?" Justin sniveled as Samantha pulled the covers up to his neck.

She saw the sad memories mix with anger in his eyes. Jessie sat up in her bed and waited patiently for the answer.

"No. I promise. We'll get up and all have breakfast together. Maybe Grampy will make pancakes again. But then Kelsie and I will have to leave and go home."

"Is it far far away?" Jessie asked. Tears welled in the corners of her eyes.

"Far away like Grandmother's, right?" Justin asked.

The words Grampy and Grandmother are about as different as the two people they represented, Samantha thought as she pulled the covers up on Jessie. Conrad had told her about how selfish his ex-wife had been when Abby and Jim had been killed. How she had let them suffer alone. And how they certainly held it against her. Would they feel the same way about her when she walked out the door tomorrow?

"No. Not as far as your Grandmother's. But yes, it's a long, long way away." She kissed them each on their foreheads. Jessie felt a little warm. Probably just from playing hard all day and the late hour.

"I changed my mind," Justin said as Samantha opened the brightly colored Sesame Street book with Grover on the cover. " I want Grampy to read my story. Not you."

"Me too," Jessie said, refusing to look at Samantha.

Samantha struggled to keep the hurt from showing on her face.

"Well, goodnight then. See you in the morning." She kissed them again before letting Conrad take her place at their bedside.

"You two apologize to Samantha. Now."

"It's okay, Conrad. Really. I understand." She walked out, turning out the overhead light as she went.

"That still wasn't very nice, but we'll talk about it tomorrow." He took a deep, ragged breath. "Okay, you guys ready to read that story about the monster we started last night?"

"Yeah. Remember Jessie, Grover was really worried about that monster. Read, Grampy. I promise we won't get scared. Honest." His tear-filled eyes followed Samantha as she left the room, belying the excitement in his voice. Then he turned back to the pages Conrad was turning.

Samantha rested against the door casing as Conrad began to read. The light from the bed side lamp reflected off the silver in his hair. She watched the love flow from Jessie and Justin's eyes to Conrad's. Thoughts of her were absent for now as they listened intently to the story. Silently, hoping they wouldn't notice that she'd been watching, she shoved herself upright and trudged down the stairs.

Chapter 34

Only the light through the half-open kitchen door filtered into the living room. Samantha stood in near darkness at the window, her mind caught up in the falling rain. Like the weatherman had predicted, the downpour was melting away the last remnants of the snow. The snowpeople they had worked so hard on had dwindled to small lumps of gray on a green-brown field of grass. She rested her forehead against the cool windowpane. What lay ahead was going to be ten times harder than she had ever dreamed.

Conrad walked quietly down the stairs. She didn't seem to hear him or see him studying her from the shadows. His chest ached to see her so miserable but he sat down on the step to watch.

She pulled a yellowed lace curtain to her nose and for a minute Conrad thought she might wipe her nose on it. Instead he saw her chest rise and fall as she inhaled the scents from his house and the people it held. Rubbing it gently against her cheek, she closed her eyes, forcing memories from the age softened fabric. Slowly she circled the room, taking in the pictures on the walls, some his, some Justin's and Jessie's. She smiled at the fancy frames unconventionally surrounding the kids primitive yet colorful paintings. No refrigerator magnets here. They, like their artists, held a place of honor in this house.

When she came to the desk, she stopped. In the dim light she studied the family portraits she had looked at so many times in the past few days. She picked up the picture of Conrad, Lisa and obviously Abby taken years before. Julia was suspiciously missing. In it Conrad's hair hung down past his collar and the Fumanchu mustache wrapped dangerously close to his mouth. Her index finger traced its path then ran across the image of Conrad's lips. Rattling the frame against the table, she set the picture down. She picked up another family photograph, this one of Abby, Jim and the children. Jessie was a baby here, the pink ruffles adding pounds to her already pudgy body. Justin was a small boy dressed in a navy blue and white sailor suit. Love and pride filled Abby's face and Jim's echoed her sentiments. Samantha's eyes clouded with tears.

Conrad stood up silently. His vision blurred as he watched her closely, trying to read what was going through her mind.

Samantha left the desk and wandered over to the couch. She stood behind it and reached for the pillow he had used that afternoon when he stretched out to watch the Carolina Panthers win another game. She clutched it to her chest then deeply inhaled his essence from the pillowcase. Forever more the scent of Canoe would bring back Conrad and the agonizing memory of losing him. Eventually she lowered her lips to the cloth and swayed back and forth to a rhythm only she could hear.

Having seen enough, Conrad walked down the rest of the steps and gently pulled the pillow from her grasp, replacing the cold lifeless replica with the warm, breathing real thing. As he lowered his lips to hers, his determination and desire grew. The kiss became deeper, longer and passion-filled.

"See, isn't this better than that old pillowcase?" his lips whispered into hers, a half smile reflecting in his eyes.

Samantha answered him by urgently seeking his lips again and again with hers. She had to let him know how she felt about him and that it wasn't for lack of caring that she would leave in the morning. She couldn't go anywhere without him conceding to that.

"Maybe we should take this upstairs," she murmured when he started to unbutton her blouse.

"Yes," was all he needed to or could say as he urgently started kissing the base of her neck.

On the way to his room, he motioned her on before he stopped and checked on the children. They were snuggled together in Justin's bed, their arms wrapped tightly around the protection of their worn stuffed animals. He knew that the next morning would be tough on them, perhaps more so than anybody else. They were younger, had lost more and hadn't learned to adjust to life's tragedies. He closed the door silently, wishing he could shelter them forever.

Opening Lisa's door he told them goodnight and that Kelsie's mom had already gone to bed.

"See you in the morning, girls."

"Dad, we're not girls. We're young ladies. Will you never, ever get it right?"

"Someday, Lisa. Maybe even before you're a grandmother. Night, ladies." A pillow hit the door as he closed it firmly behind him, wishing for the first time that there was a padlock on the outside of Lisa's room.

Samantha waited quietly at Conrad's bedroom doorway though her body was quivering in anticipation. He reached for her hand and led her into his private world. This was the one room in the house she hadn't been invited to inspect.

He had obviously taken the time and energy to fix it up for himself, with no signs of Julia or anything in the least bit feminine. She looked around at the red, navy and hunter green tartan plaid curtains and coverlet. The dark green flannel sheets looked warm, masculine and inviting. Conrad took the skeleton key from its hook and noiselessly locked the door.

Samantha felt like the proverbial virgin entering the sultan's tent until Conrad lifted her chin and passionately reminded how badly they both needed to be here, now, tonight. He picked her up and carried her over to the bed, laying her down beneath him. They struggled to remove their own and each others clothing, letting the various pieces lay wherever they landed.

Enveloped in heated desire, Samantha suddenly sat up.

"Can we turn off the lights."

"Now why would we want to go and do that?" Conrad asked, an indolent smile mixed with the lust showing plainly on his face.

"Because I don't have the body of a nineteen year old anymore and I'd just as soon you not see it too clearly. Bearing children has left me with a little unnecessary fat and a few nasty stretch marks; the little-advertised joys of motherhood."

"Thank heaven for imperfection. And I want to see every inch of what I'm getting."

"Well, I agree with the 'every inch' part, but does it have to be so bright and revealing?"

He let his eyes caress her body for a long moment before turning on a small lamp by the bed and turning off the glaring overhead light.

"Is that better?"

"UmHmmmm," she breathed as she lay back in the provocative glow, reaching for him. But this time he skirted her grasp.

"Just a second." He walked into his bathroom and came out carrying a packet of condoms. "Since we haven't had a chance to get a blood test, I think this might be a good idea."

"Thank you."

He sat on the edge of the bed and Samantha pulled herself up beside him, nakedness forgotten for the moment.

Taking her hands in his he said "I haven't done a lot of sleeping around, but before Julia left she managed to biblically know about half of the men in these parts. I didn't know about it until afterwards. Then they came out of the woodwork, so to speak, to tell me all about how lucky I was that she'd left and how many times they'd slept with her. Like knowing what a tramp she really was would make me glad she was gone. When she was home for the funeral she told me the guy she went to California with had died of AIDS. She insisted he had caught it after he left her but I don't know if she was lying or not. Since she's been gone I've only slept with a few women and I've always been careful. How about you? Anything I should know about?"

"In my whole life I've only slept with one man. Funny, sex didn't seem to mean much to me then. Maybe it had something to do with the alcohol. Do you think I knew you'd come along someday and make it all right and beautiful?"

Conrad blushed and worried about his ability to live up to Samantha's expectations.

She took the condom packet out of his hand, turning it over while she examined it.

"How old is this, anyway?"

"I stopped at Gatlinburg Drugs and bought three right after I dropped you off at your motel that first night."

She looked at him with amazement. "Pretty doggone confident weren't you?"

"No, just very hopeful and like any good Boy Scout 'be prepared' is my motto."

"All right, Eagle Scout. Bring your body over here so we can see if your uniform fits." She giggled as he pushed her back on the bed.

"Shhh. You better keep quiet unless you want an audience. Don't forget Lisa's room is right next door."

"Do you think our parents are doing it?" Kelsie asked Lisa after they heard the soft voices from the room next door where supposedly only Conrad was getting ready for bed.

"What do you think?"

Seconds passed before Kelsie asked, "Have you? Done it, I mean."

"Not quite, but Rod and I mess around sometimes. Nothing real serious yet but we get pretty close sometimes. How about you?"

"Nah. If a guy only wants one thing, then I don't hang out with him. Whenever a guy starts wanting to get close, I seem to get scared and back off. I'm not sure why, maybe because Mom had to get married way back when and she harps on me constantly about not letting that happen to me."

"Boy, don't I know about that."

They both grew quiet, trying not to listen to sounds from the other room. Finally Kelsie got up and turned up the volume on the television, though it only made her ears strain when she heard a distinctly feminine giggle.

"I hate thinking about what they're doing. Don't you? Doesn't it bother you to think of your Dad naked with my Mom? Dis-gus-ting!"

"If you weren't leaving in the morning we'd both have to get used to it, I think." Lisa held her hand up in front of her eyes, admiring the purple polish she was painting on her nails. "They're adults, Kels. Don't you want them to be together?"

"No! Yes! Oh, hell, I don't know." Frustration filled her eyes.

Lisa walked over to the other bed and sat beside Kelsie. Her arm wrapped around Kelsie's back.

"It's okay, Kelsie."

"But how do we know they won't end up hating each other?"

"I don't think your mom is going to let that happen. I think she's too afraid."

"Me too," Kelsie had to admit.

They rested their heads together and tried to concentrate on the movie.

Samantha nestled her head in the crook of Conrad's arm as they spooned on the soft sheets. His other arm draped around her waist and his fingers played lazily with her nipple.

"We seem to be a good fit, don't you think?" Conrad asked, nipping at the nape of her neck.

"Um hmmm," she agreed. "In more ways than one."

"Now I know what they say is true."

"What's that?"

"That abstinence makes the heart grow fonder."

"I think that's supposed to be absence, silly," she said, a huge smile breaking across her face. She kissed his bicep then licked it softly.

A low groan escaped from Conrad's throat. "You better stop that or you'll be sorry."

She rolled over and ran her tongue up one side of his neck, to his mouth and down the other side, teasing and tempting him with her lips and teeth as her head lowered to his chest.

"So, make me sorry," she whispered into the downy hairs on his chest.

"Do you think the girls heard?" she whispered a few wickedly playful minutes later.

"What's to hear?" He flashed her a wicked grin. "Unless you think they heard you moan when I touched you here." His hand snaked up her legs and she instantly moaned involuntarily. "I thought there would be teeth marks in the sheets. Or maybe they heard me panting your name before I collapsed. Other than that, I think we were pretty quiet."

She braced herself up on one elbow, waiting for him to open his eyes.

"Are you the silver tongued devil Kristofferson sings about?" she asked innocently. "The one who can sweep a lady off her feet before she knows what's happening?"

Conrad stuck out his tongue and tried to answer through its thickness. "Doeth it look thilver?"

Samantha impulsively flicked it with her own. "Yes, I think it truly does." Quiet laughter preceded tickling until all was relatively silent again.

He leaned away from her and opened the nightstand drawer bringing out a bottle of lavender body oil.

"Don't tell me you bought that at Gatlinburg Drugs too."

"You know, it's hell coming from a small town like this. I'll bet Clem will still have that silly smirk on his face next time I go in there even if it's not for another six months. And it may be that long before I work up the nerve to face him again."

As he opened the bottle and poured some of the oil into his hand, she rolled onto her back. Her body already yearned for him, aching for his tender touch. Rubbing his hands together he began to massage the tiny white stretch marks that ran up the side of her midriff. His hands made bigger and bigger circles, kneading her skin and muscles until she begged him to pour some oil into her hands so she could bring him into the ecstasy.

When they were both slippery and charged as electric eels, Conrad pulled out the second condom. The lubrication took them to a higher plane of erotica and afterwards, exhaustion. Within half an hour they were both sound asleep wrapped snugly in each others arms.

Chapter 35

The incessant lighthearted chirping of a cardinal woke Conrad shortly after daybreak. Though heavily overcast and dreary, light filtered in through the unshaded window. He rolled on his side to watch Samantha as she slept. Her hands rested near her mouth and he remembered how Jessie did that when she tried to stop sucking her thumb at bed time. He wondered if her fears had once been pacified by a friendly thumb. Raising his hand he brought his fingers up to stroke the velvety skin of her cheek.   Though he stopped himself before making contact, she must have sensed his closeness. She tossed around, exposing the mounds of both breasts before she lay still again, dead to the world. The view was more arousing than Conrad could handle and he rolled onto his back, breathing heavily and adjusting himself under the flannel sheet.

Samantha woke up slowly minutes later. The afterglow of incredible love making fogged her memory and she came awake happier than she could remember ever being. It took her a minute to recall where she was, what she had to do today and why. When she did, her mood plummeted and she modestly pulled the covers half way up her chest. She turned to find Conrad's eyes wide open, staring at the ceiling. Irrationally she was hurt that he hadn't felt the need to watch her nakedness. Maybe if he truly wanted her to stay, he would have rolled over and proven it. She forced herself to quiet the monsters of self doubt, knowing that Conrad truly cared for her. He had proved that in many ways in the past few days, and again through their night of little sleep and much passion. Of course he wanted more than anything for her to stay. Didn't he?

"Good morning," she said, rolling into the pit of his arm and letting the covers fall away. But when she slipped her hand under the sheet, he stole his arm from under her and folded both hands behind his head, examining the ceiling as if life's answers might lay in the swirling plaster.

Minutes passed in agonizing silence. She waited for him to say something, anything. Finally she spoke.

"If only there was some way I could make you understand," she said, pushing her body and mind away from the ache of his coolness.

"Try."

She glanced at him, looking for sarcasm but finding only pain. When he finally looked at her, he seemed to be waiting to hear her reasons, so she turned away from the distraction of his eyes and began.

"Okay. I'll try."

"That's all I ask."

There was so much that she wouldn't be able to put into words. But, for both of their sakes, she had to give him her reasons.

"See, I've always belonged to somebody. Somebody's child, somebody's wife, somebody's mother. When I was fourteen I told my Mom that when I graduated I was going to travel across the country, just like Todd and Buzz on "Route 66". Do you remember that show? They were so happy-go-lucky. Even when bad things happened to them, all they had to do is get in the car and leave them behind. That sounded like the ideal life. Unrealistic sure, but then I was only fourteen. Mom could hardly keep from laughing as she told me what a silly idea it was, that girls didn't do those things. Not proper girls, anyway. Now I realize she was only trying to protect me.

"Whatever the logic, that was the day I decided if I couldn't have my dream, I might as well get married and have babies, just like everybody else. Only I didn't plan on starting a family quite so soon."

Samantha stopped, turning her body away from Conrad's. But he pulled her backwards into his spoon, letting her have her privacy but keeping her close. He ran his hand leisurely up and down the silky skin of her hip.

She grabbed his hand and held it tightly at her waist, allowing herself to concentrate on what she wanted to say instead of the warmth that coursed through her veins when he touched her.

"The last thing I wanted to do was get married when I was seventeen, but that's what happened. Me. Quiet, shy little me. Pregnant." She shuddered twenty five years later at the horrible humiliation she had felt at the time. "He was only eighteen and almost as much a child as I was, probably more so. What a way to start a marriage. Suddenly I became a wife and a mom. I raised Jeff alone basically, since David had other priorities. I lived for that child. Time passed and I grew up. Jeff grew up. Even David grew up in some ways.

"He never hit me. Sometimes I thought it would be easier if he had. Instead he simply made sure I knew he wasn't happy with me, no matter what I did. Why wasn't I thinner, prettier, smarter? At night, when I couldn't sleep, I would tell myself someday it would be my turn to do what I wanted. Kelsie came along and I adjusted. She was always my little girl, my buddy. We were so close.

"Things got better for a while, then worse." Samantha hesitated, trying to decide if she should tell him the rest.

"And?"

"And when I started looking for just the right sized oak tree to drive into, I knew I had to go."

"Oh, Samantha," Conrad whispered, imagining how different this morning would have been if she had taken the other way out.

"I've never been sorry I left, not even for a single day. It's been rough but in a year and a half Kelsie will be eighteen and out of school. Neither one of my children will need me anymore. Then it will be my turn."

"To do what Samantha? What's so important that you've been able to keep it waiting this long?" Conrad had pulled her closer during her story, her pain dissipating into his body. "I think I have the right to ask."

After thinking about how to explain it she began again. "I've never been on my own, free to do whatever I want. I went from my father's house to my husband's house. I never had a chance to figure out who I was. When David and I divorced, I figured I finally had my chance. I've learned a lot in the past couple of years, but I've still been a mom. When Kelsie graduates I'm going to take off and be alone for a while. It's something I've dreamed about my whole life. I'll be free to do whatever I want, whenever I want. No one to tell me not to be foolish. Who knows, maybe I'll even get a second mortgage on my house, buy an old Vette and cruise from coast to coast. On my grown-up days all I want is to open my own store and sell things I love. To go to auctions and buy more goodies. But either dream means being able to do what I want. Not what someone else wants me to do."

Samantha rolled over and watched Conrad's face, inches from her own. He wouldn't give her the pleasure of meeting her eyes.

"I need you to understand. Please, Conrad. Please." Tears choked her voice.

Conrad finally kissed away the tears running down her cheeks.

"I'd always let you be free. Don't you know that? I wouldn't hold you back from anything you wanted to do."

"I know. And I was willing to make adjustments if I could have you in my future. I figured you might need the freedom as much as I did. We could take off and be foolish together, partners forever. But up there at the motel you introduced me to your world. If I was to be part of it, my dreams would be squashed again. I can't let that happen. I can't."

When she regained control of her voice, she whispered, "Please don't hate me, Conrad. I'm so sorry. Honest to God, if there was any other way, I'd take it. But I know I'd only grow to resent you and those children."

Conrad rolled over on his back, his arm still under her shoulder.

"I wish I could hate you. It would be so much easier to watch you walk away. I hated Julia when she left. Anger was the only thing that kept me going for a while. I won't even have that when you leave."

Samantha draped her leg over his and pulled herself close, the inside of her naked thigh against his hip.

She kissed his lips pulling him closer, hoping to replace this new faraway feeling with the sensual closeness they had enjoyed last night.

"You want it both ways, don't you Sam. I suppose I should feel flattered that you're willing to share your body with me." Conrad reached over on the nightstand and grasped the corner of the last condom.

"One left. Why waste it, right?" His anger showed as he ripped open the package. After rolling it on he pulled her crudely over on top of him, thrusting himself into her unready body. She gasped at the pain, but before they separated for the last time they were clinging to each other, both wishing they could find a way to never let go.

Chapter 36

Jessie opened the door and came in as they were silently making the bed.

"I thought you locked..."

"So did I."

But Jessie seemed to think nothing of the fact that Samantha was in Conrad's room, that neither one of them had on a stitch of clothing or the fact that no one was speaking. Her face was an unhealthy, rosy pink.

"Grampy?" she said rubbing her eyes sleepily. "I don't feel too pretty good."

Conrad quickly pulled on his jeans while Samantha picked her nightgown up off the floor and drew it over her head.

Sitting on the edge of the bed, Conrad carefully pulled Jessie onto his lap. Samantha covered both of them with a quilt.

"What's the matter, baby? Tell Grampy where it hurts."

"All over. My head and my tummy too."

"You're pretty hot."

"No I'm not. I'm cold, cold, cold." Sick as she was, she only had eyes for Conrad.

"Here, you sit with Sammy for a minute while I call Doc Sullivan." He handed the blanketed bundle to Samantha and she held Jessie close, rocking her with a soft swaying motion, murmuring pacifying words in her ear.

A few minutes later he came back, trying to hide a worried expression.

"Well, Jessie, Doc Sullivan said you were a smart little girl not to get sick while it was snowing. He wants us to come see him. He thinks it's the flu, but he wants to be sure. Come on, let's get you dressed." He picked her up from Samantha's lap and was half way out the door before turning to ask, "Do you want to ride along? We can pick up your car on the way back."

"Sure. I want to hear she's okay anyway. Give me five minutes to get dressed and tell Kelsie to get her stuff around."

"Hurry, Grampy, bathroom!" Jessie's hand flew to her mouth. They took off running. Samantha started to follow then stopped midstep. They could handle this without her, as they always had, as they always would.

"Pick your favorite, honey." Doc Sullivan held the gift-wrapped surprise box for her. Jessie couldn't make up her mind between the rubbery finger monster with wiggly hands or the big-footed puff ball. Finally, she picked the downy puff ball, and rubbed it against her cheek. She grasped Conrad's hand tightly in hers.

"She should be fine by this time tomorrow." Doc said as he handed the finger puppet to Jessie with a smile. "Just give her lots of juice and TLC. Hey, by the way, is that your new lady friend in the waiting room? The one I missed meeting in church yesterday?"

"That's Sammy," Jessie answered for him. "She's got a daughter named Kelsie. They're our friends. We been sleddin' and makin' snowmen and...and popcorn. But they got to go home today. They came from way far away. We're gonna miss them, ain't we, Grampy?"

"Surprising how much she talks when Justin isn't around." Doc said to Conrad. "Too bad about the friend though. Everyone at evening worship was saying how they'd like to get to know her better and that they hoped maybe she'd stick around."

"Yeah, me too Doc," Conrad said. "Me too."

Samantha stood when they entered the waiting room. Conrad introduced them.

"Nice to meet you. I was just tellin Conrad here that..."

"We gotta get home, Doc. See you Sunday. Thanks." He picked up Jessie and carried her to the car.

They stopped for Samantha's car and she made sure she didn't lose sight of Conrad's van as she followed him through the twists and turns to his house.

"Now you gotta go, huh," Jessie said when Conrad had her settled on the couch with a blanket, pillow and rag doll.

"Yep, pretty soon."

"Will you come back and see us?"

How can I answer that, Samantha wondered. Do I break her heart now or later?

"I don't know. Maybe someday."

"Hey, sweety. What do you want for breakfast? Cream of Wheat will warm that tummy. How does that sound?" Conrad tried to change the subject.

"Grampy, I hate that stuff when I feel good. You don't think I'm gonna eat it when I'm sick, do you?" Jessie giggled weakly.

"How about some toast? With a little strawberry jam on it?" Samantha asked. "Would that settle your insides down?"

"Will you make it for me?"

"Sure. Coming right up."

"You can go help her if you want, Grampy. I be okay by myself. You're a good jam spreader."

"What did Doc say?" Lisa asked as soon as they came into the kitchen. The rest of the kids sat at the table finishing up their breakfast. The counter top was completely trashed with eggs shells, toast crumbs and sausage drippings.

"He figured it was the twenty-four hour flu," Conrad answered. "He said she needs to stay quiet so that means no rough-housing today, Justin."

"Is there anything we can do before we go?" Kelsie asked between mouthfuls of sausage.

"Nah, he said just lots of tender loving care and she'd be fine." Conrad glanced over his shoulder at Samantha who stood waiting for the toast to pop up. "I guess we all could use a little of that," he muttered to himself, turning away to pour some apple juice into Jessie's Barney cup.

Chapter 37

"You're a selfish bitch!"

"A selfish bitch? I'm a selfish bitch? How dare you call me selfish when all you want is a 'Grammy' for those kids?"

The walk had started out friendly enough. When they had told everyone that they were going out for a walk in the rain, it was suspected that they were losing their minds. This was no warm spring rain. Had the temperature been ten degrees colder they would have been snowed in for weeks yet.

But they needed to talk privately one more time before they parted; after that morning, after last night. Conrad had dug up two badly wrinkled yellow rain parkas from a long ago trip to Sea World.

The tension between them built as they talked about how life would go on after their paths split. Conrad grew more and more agitated as Samantha forced herself to talk cheerfully about her Christmas plans and how many Santas she still needed to finish.

They both knew that what they were saying to each other now wasn't true. Samantha was not a selfish bitch. Conrad was not only looking for a 'Grammy' for the kids. But still they kept hurling insults, as if they needed to drive a stake through their hearts and their love.

Conrad planted his cold, wet hands firmly on each of her shoulders, holding her at arms length from him. "You come to town, bent on picking up a man, any man. Then you treat me like I'm a two bit..."

"I never..." Samantha furiously tried to break away from his hold but wasn't strong enough.

"You play your little games with me and my family. Play with our affections then pick up your bags and be on your merry way. La de da, nothing's changed. Dammit, Samantha. It's not fair. You can't do that with people."

Samantha forced her way a step closer. "You flatter yourself that I came down here intentionally to 'pick you up' as you so aptly put it. Yeah, I came looking for some great sex, and damned if I didn't get it. Now I can go home. And I'm having a ball with the fact that you're hurting. Sure, and in a few minutes I'm going to get in my car and drive away from you and your family. Then Kelsie and I are going to have a good laugh. Ha ha ha. Well, I guess you're right, Conrad. I must be a selfish bitch. But if you believe all that for one minute, then what I say is true too. You are only looking for a grandmother slash mother for those kids."

"Oh yeah, right. Like I don't care. What has it been these past few days? What was last night?"

"The past few days were fun for all of us. Last night was plain old fashioned horniness. Pure and simple. On both of our parts."

Conrad tightened his grip on her shoulders until her eyes flinched. He forced himself to loosen his fingers.

"Dammit, Samantha. Sure those kids could use a woman in their lives, but we do alright by ourselves. We don't need anybody's help. And we sure as hell don't need you."

Samantha wrenched her shoulders away from his hands and ran down to the swollen creek that flowed at the bottom of the hill. Slipping on a pile of soggy leaves, she fell to her knees in the mud.

Conrad stalked up behind her and thrust his hand out to help her. She twirled away from him, slipped twice more in the muck then stood up on her own. Glaring at the water, concentrating hard on how it swirled over the rocks, she ignored him and everything else in his stupid world.

Standing behind her with his arms crossed firmly on his chest, bitterness seeped from every pore. He would tell her he loved her now if he thought that might change things. He was ready and he knew it was true, but why give her that power since she was leaving anyway? Nothing he could say would stop her. Nothing would make one bit of difference.

"Come on. You're soaked. Let's get back to the house."

"Go to hell," she screamed at the top of her lungs. She rubbed the back of her hand across her cheeks, smearing them with mud. "Go away. Leave me alone. Tell Kelsie to put my bags in the car and I'll meet her there. Go on, tell her."

"Oh for crying out loud, Samantha, don't be an idiot. Let's go in and get you a hot shower. You'll feel better and look a hell of a lot better." He feebly smiled at her. The fight was gone out of him. It was over. Soon she'd be out of his life forever, so he might as well start getting used to it.

She didn't feel the cold raindrops as they made rivulets down her cheeks. Looking long and hard at his face, she took a mental picture for the photo album in her mind. In a few minutes she would leave here and go back to her normal, boring everyday life. Eventually, he'd be merely a pleasant memory. She would enjoy thinking about this wonderful time while she put the finishing touches on her future. Someday she might even be able to laugh at the way he looked with the rain dripping off his nose. But not today. She reached out for his hand rubbing the grit from hers into the soft skin between his thumb and forefinger.

He pulled her hand up and drew it to his lips, watching her face as he kissed her knuckles. Not getting the response he needed, he let it drop and turned back towards the house without a word. He was almost to the door before she silently started to follow, irrationally aching for him to turn around and come back to get her.

"What are Grampy and Sammy doing outside?" Justin stood at the back door watching them.

"Talking," Lisa answered from beside him.

"About what?"

"I don't know. Adult talk."

"They're getting awful wet, ain't they?"

"Yes, they are."

"Grampy'd get mad at me if I stayed out in the rain that long. Think I should call them in?"

"No. They'll be okay. They've got the ponchos on so only their heads are getting wet."

"I don't know. Grampy looks pretty sorry out there, and Sammy's all mud. Oh oh, here he comes."

Lisa drew Justin back just in time as Conrad stormed through the door, making the glass rattle as he slammed it behind him. He didn't see the looks on their faces as he made his way upstairs to the shower, leaving muddy bootprints across the linoleum and on each step.

"See, I told you so."

Samantha came up on the porch and braced herself against the door casing as she removed her shoes and socks. They were muddy beyond recognition. She looked at the shoes, at her blanched white feet, at the outside faucet. Barefoot, she carried her shoes and socks to the spigot and rinsed most of the mud away. Then she hooked up the hose and rinsed herself from head to toe.

"Ooohhh, she's gonna be in trouble. Grampy's gonna be mad when he finds out she was outside playing in the water."

"Shhh. Let's go make some hot cocoa. I think they're gonna need it."

They met in the upstairs hallway. Samantha had a towel turbaned around her head and his terrycloth robe tied tightly around her waist. Shivers still ran through her body and the worst came when Conrad stepped in front of her with only his jeans on. He had decided to use the shower downstairs and his hair was still wet, shiny and curly. Slowly rubbing a towel across his chest, he watched Samantha come towards him.

She couldn't stand looking at him this way. He looked too good, too vulnerable, too...

"Excuse me," she said softly, lowering her head as she forced her feet to walk past him.

He flattened himself against the wall, avoiding contact as if she had leprosy or something equally contagious. He tried to keep his eyes on the floor too, but they followed her retreating figure into the bedroom and watched her back as she closed the door.

Chapter 38

By noon their suitcases were at the door. All that was left was saying goodbye. Kelsie and Lisa talked quietly in the corner for a while then joined the others. Conrad plastered on a fake smile so Samantha did too. Jessie cried when she picked her up, wrapping her arms and legs around Samantha's middle.

"Bye bye, Sammy," she whispered into her ear.

Samantha cleared her throat before she answered. She hugged Jessie close, wishing there was some way she could make this easier. Maybe she shouldn't have let her get so close. Maybe she should have stayed aloof for the sake of the crying child nuzzling her neck so desperately. She caught Conrad's eye from across the room. He watched them for a moment, then turned his back on her and looked out the window.

"I'll really miss you, Sweety. Get feeling better, and take care of your Grampy, okay?"

"Okay," was all Jessie could answer as crocodile tears streaked her cheeks. Lisa left Kelsie's side and pulled Jessie gently into her arms.

Justin stood in the dining room doorway, his face looking like a thundercloud ready to burst. Samantha knelt in front him.

"Don't be mad, Justy. Please. I have to go home. I have a job and a dog and a house."

Justin wouldn't say a word. He stood with his arms crossed, proud and unbending as a cigar store Indian.

"I do care about you. You know that don't you? But I have to go. Please, let's be friends. Okay?"

No amount of cajoling would get him to speak. Conrad took her arm and hauled her up. "He'll be fine once you're gone," he said then softened the rudeness of the statement with, "You know how kids are."

"I know," she said, standing but keeping her eyes on the solemn little boy before her. "Bye bye, Justin."

He continued to glare straight ahead, refusing to let his eyes meet Samantha's. A single tear brimmed in each eye, the only clue to his emotions. With a kiss to the top of his head, Samantha turned and walked out on the porch.

When Kelsie tried to kid around with him, he refused to have anything to do with her too. Eventually she shrugged her shoulders and joined Lisa and Jessie.

"So you'll come down and visit us next summer when school's out?" Lisa asked Kelsie quietly so Samantha wouldn't hear. "Remember, Rod's folks have that place out on the river and a bunch of tubes. We always have a lot of fun out there. It would be great if you could stay all summer. Besides, that kid I introduced you to, Nathan, hangs around Rod a lot. And I know you could find a job in town. Wouldn't that be great?"

"Yeah, but I'll wait a while before I mention it to Mom. I don't know how she'd feel about us staying friends."

"I know what you mean," Lisa said as she watched Conrad and Samantha try to ignore each other. "I really thought I was going to get a baby sister out of this deal."

"Baby sister? I'm only seven months younger than you. I don't think that qualifies for 'baby sister'. Do you?"

They both laughed as they hugged each other.

"I'm going to miss you. I would have liked being your sister," Kelsie continued. She looked at the glowering couple on the porch. "And they call us children."

"Just go," Conrad said, trying to look nonchalant as he leaned on the porch railing. "Get on with your life and I'll get on with mine. The sooner you leave, the better off we'll all be. Bye, see ya, adios."

"Fine. Come on Kelsie, let's get out of here before we get booted out." She glared at Conrad who stepped out of her way, then helped carry their bags to the car. Lisa held Jessie at the window. Nearing the car Kelsie held out her hand for the keys. She was amazed when Samantha tossed them to her.

Samantha looked around one last time. The only things left of the snowpeople they had built were the bright orange carrots, pieces of black rock and pinecones lying in the mud. The red bow had blown across the yard and lay against a dirty snow drift that was taking its time to melt in the cold rain. The spot where they had made angels in the snow was once again only soggy, dying grass. There were no tracks from the sleigh Petal had pulled up this driveway. The mountains were dark and dreary now that their snowy winter coat had melted. It didn't seem so magical to her today and she futilely hoped the snow was the only hold this place had on her.

Kelsie impulsively threw her arms around Conrad's neck.

"I'm glad we finally became friends," he said into her ear, barely above a whisper. "Take good care of your Mom."

"I will. I'm sorry I was such a brat to you at first. You're okay, for an old hillbilly." Her smile wavered. "Justin will be okay, won't he?"

"He'll be fine. I talked to him this morning and tried to explain everything to him, but he still can't believe he's losing somebody special again. Actually, neither can I."

Kelsie tightened her grip around Conrad's neck. "I wish I could help somehow but Mom's pretty stubborn when she wants to be." She reached up and kissed his grizzled cheek. "I'll work on her."

Conrad let her go then went around to the other side of the car where Samantha stood. He hugged her briefly. After a quick peck on the cheek he turned away and headed for the house. He was halfway there and Samantha had one leg in the car before he turned around and came back. She rejoiced and cringed at the same time.

"I'm not going to make this easy for you, Samantha Jean. I'm going to make you suffer with your decision as much as I do." He glanced over at Kelsie and gave her a solemn wink, then turned back and walked to the house without another word.

She watched him go, wanting to call out to him but knowing she couldn't. They climbed into the car and had started to pull away when they heard a loud banging noise. The plate glass window quivered as Justin pounded on it, waving furiously. They waved back and blew kisses to him.

"I'm not gonna cry. I'm not gonna cry," Samantha chanted as they drove down the driveway. She kept her word until they reached the road. Even Kelsie had tears in her eyes as she watched in the rearview mirror as the old farm house receded into the distance.

PART

TWO

Chapter 1

Conrad stood in the open doorway, his restraining hands on Justin's shoulders as watched the car retreat down the driveway. He wondered if maybe he should chase after her, running and screaming like a madman. Maybe he should have chained her to the basement wall and kept her on bread and water until she came around to his way of thinking. These thoughts, the sane and the insane, raced through his mind as he watched them turn right at the road. He stared at the curve where he last saw her car, wondering how he could have let her go.

"Dad, you're letting all the heat out." Lisa was beside him gently pulling him in the house and closing the door behind him. "Come on. It's nap time. You take Jessie, I'll take Justin. Dad? Dad?"

When Lisa pushed Jessie into his arms, Conrad forced his mind out of the slime-filled crater it had been swimming in.

"Can we have a story before we go to sleep?" Jessie asked as they climbed the stairs to their room.

"Not today, Jess. Grampy has a headache. Okay?"

Jessie pouted. "Sammy woulda read to me."

Watching Conrad's thunderous look, Lisa told Jessie she would read to them. "But you'll have to take a good nap afterwards. Pick out a book while I get your water. Make it a short one, though."

"Thanks," Conrad said, depositing Jessie on her bed. "I think I'll go stretch out for a minute myself. Call me if you need me." He kissed Lisa on the forehead then trudged into his room.

He lay flat on his back, his eyes unfocused. Yet he couldn't close them. When he did, thousands of frames flickered through his head like an old silent movie. Not bothering to take his shoes off, dirt from the driveway smeared the quilt. There was a hollowness in the pit of his stomach that no food could fill.

Valiantly he tried to figure out how he could make it all work. Maybe Jim's parents had changed in this past year. Maybe they needed some company, someone to love and care for. Maybe they would take the kids for a while now. Give him and Samantha a chance to have some time alone. Maybe they could get away from here for a while, just the two of them. Lisa could stay with friends and…he stopped in mid thought.

"Don't be an idiot," he chided himself. None of this would work and he knew it. He didn't even want it to, really. He would never give those kids up to Jim's parents, not even for a day. And Lisa still needed him to help finish her transition from child to adult. He rolled over and put his nose against the pillow at his side, inhaling the scent of her cologne and the body oil they had used the night before. Maybe he would wait a while before he washed the bedding. But he highly doubted he would ever pull the covers back and sleep under them again. Samantha had been there and now she wasn't.

"Mom? Mom, are you ready to drive yet? All this rain's making me a little sleepy."

Samantha slowly turned her head away from the window that she had held her full attention for over two hours. Her eyes were red rimmed but the tears had stopped long ago. She looked around as if coming out of a trance. "Where are we?"

"Almost to Corbin."

Samantha was completely disoriented. "Did we go through Knoxville already?"

"Over an hour ago."

"Oh, Kelsie, I'm so sorry. Why didn't you say something?"

"I did okay. Besides, I figured we were better off with me at the wheel. At least my mind was on the road."

"Let's hit that," Samantha said after a long silent minute, pointing to a billboard for a Burger King a mile up the road. "I could stand something cold to drink. Then I'll drive."

"You sure you're up to it? I can drive some more after we take a break. I'm a little sleepy, that's all."

Samantha gently stroked the back of Kelsie's head. "You're a good kid."

Kelsie grinned into the rearview mirror as she flicked on the turn signal. "Yeah, I am, aren't I?"

The room was dark when Conrad finally pulled himself together. The sounds of pans rattling drifted up from the kitchen below. He turned on the bedside lamp, its sultry light momentarily recalling the night with Samantha. The clock said 6:30 and he knew he that, though he was sure he hadn't slept, he had lost six hours of his life. He brushed the dried mud off the foot of the bed then went down to see about supper for the kids.

"Hi. Guess I fell asleep," he said when he entered the kitchen. Lisa noticed his eyes looked haunted instead of rested, but she didn't say a word. Justin came over and climbed on his lap as soon as he sat down.

"Lisy's making pancakes and eggs. Is that all right? I told her you might not like having breakfast at bed time but she said I shouldn't worry so much. Won't our tummies be confused, Grampy?"

"No, pancakes and eggs sound fine. Thanks Lisa. What can I do to help?"

"Pour drinks if you want. Justin and Jessie set the table, so that's about all there's left to do."

Conrad sat Justin down in his chair. As he took down the glasses down from the cupboard, his eyes fell on a used cup in the sink. Samantha's cup. Her pale coppery lipstick still coated the edge. He picked it up and ran his thumb along the smear.

"Don't use that one, silly. It's dirty," Justin said at his side. "Here's a clean one. Do you want Lisy to make a pot of coffee?"

For the first time Samantha didn't pay any attention to the tobacco-blackened barns of Kentucky or the simple wooden fences surrounding the prosperous horse farms. About all that did register from the outside world was a suspicious-looking semi whose trailer appeared to have been modeled after a tank, sturdier and heavier than most of the trucks flying past them on the down-side of these hills. This truck seemed to lumber more like an overweight prehistoric beast. Something green and ominous oozed from around the edges, poisonous and possibly life threatening. For some reason, it seemed to be in keeping with the way her mind and heart was reeling.

They fought a bitter wind most of the way home. Rain blew almost sideways and by the time they pulled up in front of their house, it was mixed with sleet.

"We'll unload later," Samantha told Kelsie. "This has got to let up soon."

"Mom, it's November. It doesn't have to 'let up' until April."

Samantha sighed heavily. "True, but let's wait and see if we don't get a break."

They dashed into the side porch and unlocked the door. Kelsie headed straight to the thermostat, cranking it up to eighty before offering to make tea and hot cocoa.

Samantha wandered around the kitchen of the place they had called home for two years. Though not a great house, she had turned this little place into a comfortable haven. Pale yellow paint and crisp white lace valances replaced the 50's pinkish tan walls and gold-ringed cafe curtains. The hunter green and white checkered floor added to the homey look.

She took the hot tea Kelsie handed her and they went into the living room. Here her eyes rested on the homemade curtains and the grapevine valance she and her friend, Marcy, had made last August. A couple of the dried flowers had fallen to the floor in her absence and she made a mental note to pick them up before she went to get Dolly from the kennel. Dolly was noted for scooping up anything that hit the floor, be it food, paper or even Smoky, the fat gray cat they had adopted a year ago.

The quiet, restful decorating had always brought her comfort after a day in the classroom. So why was it failing her? Why couldn't she feel at peace now when she needed it most?

"I'm pooped," Kelsie announced, plopping into the over-stuffed chair near the television. "I think I need a nap."

"Sounds like a great idea. Tomorrow's going to be a rough day, what with school and all. Let's take it easy for the rest of the day. Later we'll find something for supper. There must be something to eat in this house."

Kelsie crossed the room and planted an unexpected kiss on her mother's cheek.

"You okay?" she asked.

"Sure, I'll be fine. Just a little tired is all."

After flashing her an unbelieving look, Kelsie half ran up the stairs. "I'm going to write a letter to Lisa. You want me to send Conrad your love?"

"No!"

Kelsie giggled then closed the bedroom door.

Stretching out on the couch, Samantha pulled the afghan up to her nose and listened to the ice pelting the rooftop. She was soon asleep, rolled up tightly in her cocoon. Her last thoughts were of Conrad and what he might be doing at this very minute in Gatlinburg.

Her dreams brought him back with a vengeance. She could see herself snuggled up on his couch; see him watching the UT football game. Her pillow became his lap and she felt his arm around her shoulder.

Rock hard disappointment gripped her stomach when she woke an hour later. Her conscious mind knew she was not at his place and would not be there no matter how hard she wished it. She lay still, refusing to open her eyes to the bitter reality. When she did, Kelsie was sitting in the rocker, reading a magazine.

"I thought you were going to sleep all day. I found a can of vegetable soup, and guess what? We've got crackers and some cheese that looks okay. All at the same time. Can you believe it?"

"Wow! How'd that happen?" She was the first to admit that organization around the house was not one of her most notable skills.

Samantha tried to concentrate on the immediate future of food and drink, but the heavenly-hellish reality of the dream blocked her thoughts.

Kelsie knew when she was being ignored.

"I guess I'll go call Jeff and Carrie. They weren't home when I tried earlier. We can start the soup when I get off the phone if you want."

"Hey, Carrie, how's it going? Still pregnant?" Samantha was able to hear Kelsie clearly though she was up in her room. Carrie was Jeff's wife, the one who was carrying her first grandchild. She listened absentmindedly to one side of the conversation and could tell when Jeff got on the phone by the different way Kelsie talked; a closer, more sister-brother way.

"Yeah, we had a good time...no, I didn't meet any wild mountain men. Well, a couple maybe but nobody I need to mention just yet...Actually, yeah, the man who's house we stayed at. Him and Mom got along real well, if you get my drift...She told you that...No, he was her age...maybe she didn't want you to worry about any hanky panky...Just a second."

Samantha heard the door close and the conversation became muffled. Tip-toeing up the steps, she stood at the top and listened shamelessly.

"Yes...no, I'm not kidding...I know they were because I could hear them through the wall...no, I wasn't trying to listen. We even turned the TV up...How should I know?"

Samantha could feel her blood pressure turning her whole body into a flaming candlewick. Scarlet skin tightened on her cheeks as the rest of her body previewed her first hot flash. She threw the door open and found Kelsie sitting on the floor, sorting through her CDs as she talked.

"Why didn't you go downstairs to watch TV or something? You could have at least had the decency to knock and tell us to quiet down. And to tell Jeff..."

"I gotta go," Kelsie said quietly as she replaced the phone in its cradle.

"Mom, I..."

Samantha turned and ran down the stairs, missing the second to the last one and landing hard on the floor beneath. She limped into the living room where she threw herself on the couch, rubbing her ankle, trying to erase the pain.

She averted her eyes when Kelsie finally worked up the nerve to come downstairs. Sitting in the most distant chair, she watched her mother warily.

"We weren't listening, or at least we weren't trying to. And we didn't actually hear anything. Just...voices. If you had been eavesdropping carefully you would have heard what I told Jeff before that. Mom, look at me."

Samantha continued to stare at a speck of lint on the carpet.

"I told him that you fell head over heels for Conrad. That if you weren't so pig-headed we'd probably be packing up and shopping for those gaudy UT sweatshirts right now."

Kelsie left the rocker and walked on her knees over to the couch. "Come on, Mom, admit it. You know deep down that you've really screwed up this time."

Kelsie was warming to the new tone of the conversation when the phone rang. She thought about letting the machine pick up but of course Jeff was on the other end.

"Hello," she said. "Jeff, I don't know if now's a good time...Okay, just a minute." She handed the phone to Samantha who looked at it as if it was a coiled rattlesnake and shook her head. "I told you so...Okay. See ya then."

"He's on his way over and he's going to bring Arby's. He wants to hear all the gruesome details...his words, not mine."

Samantha rolled into the fetal position, moaned and buried her face in the pillow. She didn't know which she hated to face the most, Jeff or the truth about how miserable she was without Conrad. She wished he could be sitting beside her while she tried to explain her love life to her son.

Jeff parked his car in front of the house and ran up the steps, slipping and sliding on the icy pellets that covered the cement. Kelsie met him at the door.

"Mom's doing her statue imitation."

Jeff looked at her, trying to decipher her meaning.

"She hasn't moved since you called. I think I'll take my supper upstairs, if you don't mind. I'm already in enough hot water."

Jeff handed her a sandwich, a bag of fries and a Coke then carried the rest into the living room.

"Mom, you sleeping or what?" No answer. "I brought food," he said, holding the french fry bag where he figured her nose must be.

He sat cross-legged on the floor in front of her and opened the first roast beef sandwich. With his mouth full he said, "What am I going to do with you?"

Samantha reached her hand out from under the covers and Jeff put a sandwich in it. She sat up, looking at everything but him as she took a small bite. Nausea hit her and she handed the sandwich back to him.

Jeff pulled himself up on the couch and sat beside her.

"Mom, whatever happened between the two of you is between the two of you. It's not my business and it's not Kelsie's. But I'm having a hard time figuring out why you came back here, unless it was to pack up and say adios. Kelsie says you were so happy but you won't go back to him. How come?"

"Right now I honestly couldn't tell you. But I'm sure I'll remember my reasons in a few days. I've got to, Jeff, or I'll go insane."

Jeff took her in his arms and held her tight as she cried out the hopeless misery that was breaking her heart.

Chapter 2

Conrad stared at the brush in his hand. There was something he was supposed to be doing with it but he couldn't quite remember what. He had brought in a couple of old sketches from home but wasn't able to figure out where to start. The piece of paper lay accusing vacant before him.

Lucile stared at him from across the room. He could tell she was feeling sorry for him and he hated that almost as much as not having Samantha there beside him. These days Lucile watched him like a hawk, probably because of the time he had hollered at the young woman who was wandering the store. But he had honestly thought that she was trying to hit on him. He had made his feelings known to the point of embarrassment on both of their parts. After that, Lucile had made sure no one of the female gender between the age of 16 and 80 came within five feet of him. She had even turned his paint table around and made him sit with his back to the window. Racks of his own paintings surrounded him so no one could get too close.

Well, he couldn't help it. It wasn't his fault that Samantha had ruined this place for him. The problem was he had shared so many of his favorite places with her and these days it was becoming hard to find a place that didn't dredge up some kind of memory of her. This included his studio, kitchen, and even his yard. And when he entered his bedroom, the place that had always been his sanctuary, his mind reeled as he recalled their night together.

There wasn't anything he could do about it, either then or now. She didn't care enough, that was all there was to it. Time to get on with it, he told himself over and over.

Finally, he gave up. Throwing the brush down on the table, he grabbed his leather coat and stalked out the door without so much as a word to Lucile.

He was ten feet down the hall before he heard her holler out from the doorway, "Richmond, stop feeling so danged sorry for yourself. It's starting to get real old."

He stopped dead in his tracks, his back to her. Finally he turned and trudged back to her, planted a kiss on her cheek, then left again without speaking.

Samantha prayed endlessly for relief. Day prayers while she walked out to recess with the kids. Night prayers while she watched the clock tick away the darkest hours. But there never was any answer.

The first Sunday after they got home she went to church. The music helped. She tried to concentrate on the sermon; something about Bethlehem and the birth of Christ, of that much she was sure. But the rest was lost to her. She didn't see the polished, gray-haired minister at the raised alter. Instead she saw a portly, balding pastor in a small country church. Instead of today's sermon she clearly heard the attributes of Conrad Richmond. The service was barely over when she jumped up and bolted from the church.

Hours were spent wandering around the house. She knew she had a ton of things to do, but was unable to concentrate on anything for more than a minute or two. She wished he'd just call to say hi, then tried to convince herself that she was glad when he didn't. Her mind vacillated back and forth at least twenty times a day and on lonely days, twenty times an hour. Call him; don't call him. Love him; don't love him. Need him; don't need him. Never an answer that would last more than an hour, never solving anything, only thinking. Constant, deep, unhealthy thinking. It had to stop and she tried to convince herself that someday it would.

She wore her Gatlinburg sweatshirt from the minute she got in the door until bedtime. It was getting more ratty by the day and Kelsie threatened to
throw it away if she ever found it when Samantha wasn't home. But it brought her a bit of comfort and these days she would take whatever she could get.

******

Chapter 3

On a night two weeks after Samantha's desertion, Conrad woke in the middle of the night with a longing worse than he'd felt since she'd left. He remembered dreaming of her laying beside him and the softness of her skin became almost tangible in his hands. She'd whispered delicate and indelicate words into his ear as she nipped at the lobes with her teeth. His sheets were clammy when he woke up and he threw them off in disgust. His need for her at that moment was mostly physical and he tossed and turned, unable to find comfort in any position.

"Samantha," he moaned aloud, but there was no answering sigh. He opened his eyes to the lonely darkness then listened for a sign that anyone had heard him call out. No one came in and the desolate silence was almost deafening in his ears.

Samantha's arms were loaded down with Christmas presents. Though the spirit was missing, she made up her mind to get her shopping done and over with. As she walked through the mall she mentally checked off names of the people she had bought for. She was deep in concentration as she passed the Victoria's Secrets shop but a flash of pale yellow satin caught her eye. She stopped to look at the gown shimmering in the candle-shaped spotlights. A low-cut sweetheart neckline pulled the fabric down to barely cover the mannequin's breasts. The straps were two inches wide and rested on the outside of the shoulders. The display was set up so the back could be seen from the side window and Samantha slowly walked around. In the back the straps crisscrossed and the side panels met low on the hips, exposing a second cleavage. Samantha stood transfixed. The most gorgeous nightgown in the world and, as usual, she had no one to wear it for.

"No one, do you hear me," she said softly to herself.

But her feet ignored her mind's command and took her to the display inside the store. There was nothing in her size in yellow but there was a fairly pretty midnight blue one. She picked up the price tag and turned it over in her hand. $99.95. Oh well, she didn't have anyone to please with it anyway.

"We've got this yellow one over here that was just brought back because the strap wasn't sewed on right," a well dressed sales lady said. "We could let you have it for $40. I'll bet you'd have to shorten it anyway."

Samantha hesitated. Why buy it? She wasn't going to be seeing Conrad again and the blue striped flannel one in Penney's would be so much more serviceable. Be realistic for a change, she insisted to herself.

"I'll take it," an imposter, using her voice, said a little too loudly.

That night, when she was alone in the house with both doors locked and Kelsie at David's for the night, Samantha stood in front of the mirror. Turning from side to side, she noticed that at least her misery was good for something. She had lost six pounds in the past couple of weeks and the change was reflected in the smooth, flowing fit of the gown. The sweetheart neckline dipped deep between her breasts exaggerating what cleavage she had.

She ran her hands across the silky cloth then sighed at the thought of how good it would feel if this were Conrad's touch instead of her own. Lowering herself to the edge of the bed, she escaped to a world of make believe. But reality hit hard when she had to admit that there was no Conrad here to cuddle with. No chest to rest her head on. No pillow talk before drifting off to sleep. No one to spoon around. All there was now was a cold bed, a lonely house and an unresponsive, frigid world.

As she hung the gown on the padded hanger, she was sure the magical aura she had hoped to find was gone. What had she expected? A hocus-pocus effect that would conjure up Conrad right there in front of her eyes?

She was so sick and tired of crying, but more tears came as she climbed back into her bed. She pulled her flannel gown down to her ankles and the covers up to her neck. Dolly jumped up on the bed and licked at her face, trying to somehow help her mistress through this pain.

She lay with her eyes wide open for what seemed like hours. When the phone rang, her first thought was to wonder who died.

"Hello?" she said anxiously into the receiver.

Conrad's deep voice came through the phone line; low and husky from lack of sleep.

"Hi, Darlin. I was dreaming about you a couple of hours ago and I couldn't get back to sleep so I thought I'd call. Did I wake you?" He didn't give her a chance to answer. "You'd be mortified if I was to tell you how realistic and wonderful the dream was, so I won't."

Samantha lay her head back on the pillow, reveling in the fact that he was missing her too. She had never wanted to hear a voice more in her life. Tonight she would give in to her true emotions. Afterall, she could always say she was half asleep and not responsible for her actions. She smiled at the phone.

"You were in my thoughts too. I couldn't get you off my mind," she admitted.

Conrad sighed with pleasure. "You miss me?"

"I always miss you." She hoped the shallow, rapid breathing that had started when she first heard his voice wouldn't be audible through the phone wires. "Anyway, I pretended you were right here with me; hands, lips...everything. I almost made myself believe it too. Almost."

He took a deep, ragged breath and told himself not to fracture the fragile bond they were sharing, if only for tonight. He must simply enjoy the sound of her voice as his mind filled with memories of her.

"I'm actually much better in the flesh," he said lightly.

"Yeah, I remember," she sighed in response.

The moment became too intense and silence thickened at ten cents a minute.

"I guess I better go." Conrad glanced at the clock by his bed. He was sure they hadn't said anything for almost fifteen minutes.

"Yeah, this is pretty expensive heavy breathing we've got going here and I've got school tomorrow."

"I know. And I've got to be down to Lucile's by 8:00. She's got some out of town folks coming in that want to talk to me about a certain scene they want painted. Good money, Lucile says."

"Well, good luck."

"Thanks. Okay if I call again sometime?"

"Yes. No! Oh, I don't know. Maybe."

Conrad chuckled. "You take care, Darlin. Love you."

The last was murmured so softly she wasn't sure if he'd said it at all.

"What? Conrad, wait a minute. What did you say?" The line was dead. Had he said it or was it only in her mind? She heard the click of the phone as he hung up and it tore like a bullet through her heart.

Damn. Where had that come from? He'd meant to say "Take care, Darlin'" and leave it at that. Why did the "love you" sneak in? Sure he'd known it for a while now. Almost knew it since the moment she'd asked if she could watch him paint. Kinda knew it when they made angels in the snow. Absolutely felt it when he plunged deep into her body. Definitely knew it when his heart broke watching her drive away. It had pounded in his heart every day, hour, and second since she'd left. But he sure hadn't meant to say it. Saying it now wouldn't do him any good. It would only make him more vulnerable in her eyes.

Well, maybe she'd hung up before he'd said it. Maybe she'd missed the words she wasn't meant to hear. Or maybe she heard them and didn't care. Or maybe she heard them and was dialing the phone back right now to say those same words to him. He waited. Waited for a sound that didn't come. He finally drifted off to a restless sleep. By morning, the whole night seemed like a dream...a wet, crazy, sad dream.

******

Chapter 4

Six naked old men sat straight-legged on the floor in front of Samantha. Their virginal, protuberant bodies matched their fluffy white hair and beards. Some smiled and some scowled. They all watched her expectantly as if waiting for her to breathe life into them.

Their Santa faces had been painstakingly molded by hand. She had worked for hours on a single nose, only to crinkle the whole thing up and start all over. Sometimes she wondered if this was how God felt when he created man, and questioned if was ever truly happy with the results.

Samantha picked up the one closest to her, straightening his bent arms. It was time to mold their personalities by picking out the colors and fabrics each would wear.

From the piles around her she began by picking out a piece of green velvet. From the next pile she pulled out a length of gold braid from the tangle of trims. She pawed through another pile, this one of buttons, snaps, and earrings. She found what she was looking for. A bright gold ball earring would make the perfect closure for the long hooded coat she would make. Finally, from the stack of accessories, she pulled out a teddy bear and a tin soldier.

She went through this process with each of the chubby Santas even though today it wasn't much fun. Usually this was her favorite part of the whole Santa-birthing process but she knew the pressure was on to finish. They should have been all dressed and ready to deliver by now. She had lost too much time in Gatlinburg, and wasted too much time wandering aimlessly since then. Now she'd have to rush to get them finished in time to fill her orders. She stayed at it for hours and sometimes whole minutes went by without a single thought of Conrad.

Chapter 5

"Grampy, come see what me and Jess made."

Conrad looked away from the rerun that his eyes, if not his mind, were glued to. The two kids had been sitting at the dining room table, quietly playing a game of Candyland. Or at least that's what he thought they were doing. He stretched before walking over to the table.

"Pretty, huh Grampy?" Jessie said as he stood behind her chair.

Justin proudly held up the paper for Conrad to see. He grabbed the edge to hold it steady while Justin's excitement squirmed through his hand.

On the 11 x 14 sheet of paper, obviously swiped from his largest sketch pad, were the words "MARRY CRISMAS, SAMI + KILSEE"

"See Grampy, it's for Sammy. Kelsie too. I wrote it and look inside here. Me and Jess made pictures. I made a reindeer and Jess made a snowman."

Conrad looked closely at the drawing, carefully confining the smile to his eyes. The reindeer's face was a 6" inch circle. Branches the size of small tree trunks sprouted from the top, swooping and swirling across Justin's side of the paper and slightly onto Jessie's. A bright red ball circled around the middle 3 inches. On the opposite side of the paper Jessie had made a small, intricate snowman. Six lopsided balls sat one atop another, cantilevered and tilting past the center crease in the page.

"Ain't it pretty. Didn't we do good?" Justin hopped up and down beside Conrad.

"I'm impressed. You guys did this all by yourselves? No elves snuck in here and helped or nothin'?"

Justin and Jessie giggled, beaming up at him.

"Nope. I even went into your room and got the paper out of your...oops. Sorry, but we had to have paper. It's okay ain't it. Just this once?"

"Yes, but next time ask."

"But we did ask, honest. You didn't hear us was all. You was watching Andy...you know, that funny one where Barney thinks he can sing."

Conrad looked closely at Justin. They had learned quickly how far away his mind was these days, and had learned to take advantage of it. Had he been watching Andy? He couldn't remember. He did that a lot lately, becoming totally involved by something that was lost to him fifteen minutes later.

"Come on, I'll help you write a big envelope."

"Can we send it tonight?"

"We'll see. Let's get it ready first."

They went through three envelopes and half an hour's work before they got one that the post office would accept. Justin had painstakingly written each letter Conrad told him to put down. He shook the cramp from his hand when Conrad finally said he was done.

"Whew, that's more work than the card. Can we go mail it now? It would fit in that big box down at the postoffice. Can we take it now? Can we please?"

Conrad looked at his watch. Seven fifteen. Bedtime was in a few minutes, but he knew no one would get any sleep until this envelope was on its way.

"Get your coats and shoes on and we'll run in quick. Jessie, bring me yours and I'll help you."

They scampered to the closet. Conrad picked up the envelope and looked at it. Quickly he scrawled a note on a back corner.

> "S. I warned you I wouldn't make it easy,
> and I'd never lie about a thing like that. C."

"Hello?" a soft voice said into the phone.

"Jessie? Is that you? This is Sammy, honey." She wondered why Jessie was answering the phone. When Jessie didn't say anything Samantha added, "I wanted to thank you for the pretty card you and Justin sent."

"Okay." Jessie smiled and twisted away from Conrad as he tried to get the phone. "It's for me," she said, covering up the mouthpiece with her tiny little hand. Conrad stood by, looking puzzled.

"Did you guys make it all by yourselves?"

"Uh huh."

"Well, you did a great job."

"Thank you."

"Don't forget to tell Justin for me. Okay?"

"Yes. Bye bye."

Samantha looked at the disconnected phone in her hand. There had been no chance to ask for Conrad or even see how he was. Maybe someday she would see how cute it was that Jessie had hung up on her, but for now it bit with disappointment.

"Who was it, Jess?"

"Sammy."

Conrad lunged for the phone, but all he got for his effort was the monotonous drone of a dial tone.

"She didn't want you, Grampy. She called for me and Justin but since he ain't here, I got to talk."

Conrad plopped back into his chair, a confused look on his face.

"I'm sorry. Did I goof again?" Jessie's bottom lip quivered.

He pulled her into his arms. "No honey, of course not. Now don't cry." They snuggled on the couch, enjoying the fact that Justin and Lisa were out shopping and they had the house to themselves. Suddenly, Conrad stood up. "Come and help me, Jess. I just thought of a way to get Sammy to call and want to talk to me."

Chapter 6

The phone rang at four in the morning. This time Conrad came into her head first. She picked it up, hoping, yet dreading, to hear his low, sleepy, ever so sexy middle-of-the-night voice on the other end.

"Hello?" she said, breathless in seductive anticipation.

"Hi, Gramma."

"Jeff? Is that you? What did you say? Gramma? Did you have the baby? What is it, boy or girl? Is everyone okay? What..."

"Mom, get a grip. Yes, we have a tiny, beautiful girl. Her name is Robyn Kay. You've got to get up here. She's the cutest little girl in the world. Carrie had a rough time. We've been here since 8:00 last night but she's okay now. Man, is it worth it though."

Samantha looked up to find a half-asleep Kelsie standing in front of her.

"It's a girl. Robyn Kay. Everyone is fine." Samantha's eyes shone in the dim bedroom light. "Throw some clothes on and let's go." She never realized that she had said goodbye to Jeff after she had already hung up the phone.

Conrad looked at the tiny envelope with the Michigan postmark. His large fingers pried at the flap, even though it was addressed to all of them. By all rights, he should have waited, knowing how little mail the kids got to open. Finally, he tore the envelope away and pulled out the small card. A picture fell to the floor, and he stooped to pick it up, hoping it would be Samantha or at least Samantha and Kelsie. But instead it was a tiny baby. Blue eyes stared up at him from a red and blotchy face with a nose definitely reminiscent of Samantha's. He read the card. Robyn Kay Evers; December 13, 1997; 7 pounds, 9 ounces; 22 inches long.

He reached for the phone then stopped. No, if she'd wanted to talk to him, she should have called instead of sending this announcement, pleasing that it was that she thought of him at all. Well, two could play at that game. He replaced the handset.

The last day before Christmas vacation was usually one of Samantha's favorites. There were presents to be exchanged, homemade cookies and cakes from the mothers, and the kids were always so happy and excited. This year, though, it was awful. The kids seemed to nag and whine and by the time she got home her head was pounding.

"What the...?" She said aloud when she saw the wide, nearly flat package leaning against the inside porch door.

She laid it on the dining room table while she took off her coat and gloves, watching it warily. Using a knife she opened one end and pulled out the contents. She figured out what it was before she had it completely free, and tore at the newspaper taped to the edges.

In front of her was the painting that brought Conrad and her together; all framed, matted and wonderful. A note was taped to the glass.

"So I lied! Merry Christmas, Samantha!"

Samantha couldn't move. The picture held her as memories invaded her mind. She clearly saw him standing in front of his table, paintbrush in hand as he magically applied this last apple, this last fleck of snow, this last rabbit track in the foreground. Her fingers traced tree limbs across the glass.

She didn't know how long she stood there. It could have been minutes and it could have been hours. When Dolly began pawing frantically at the back door, she leaned the picture carefully against the table leg and hooked Dolly's leash in her collar.

Returning after their evening walk, she resolutely decided she would pick the painting up, hang it on the wall and not spend the rest of her life thinking about its painter. It was a beautiful rendition of a wonderful scene painted by a tall handsome artist and that was all. It would brighten her living room...as Conrad could have and quite possibly should have brightened her life.

Picking up the frame, she noticed a large envelope taped to the back. It was cruel enough for him to send this picture; hard telling what form of torture he had put in the envelope. Consciously afraid, she opened it slowly and drew out a much smaller painting.

She let her knees buckle her to the floor as she gazed into it, gradually taking in its meaning.

Darkness was interrupted by what appeared, at first glance, to be helter-skelter pinpoints of light. Finally she noticed a pattern; they were the lights of the arches near the iron bridge. Where they had tried to make sense out of what was happening to them. The bridge where he had tenderly given her the first of not nearly enough kisses.

Snow covered the ground as it had not done that night, and falling flakes reflected the lights. Through misted vision she saw dark patches on the ground and made out the shadows of two intertwining bodies, the lips above them meeting passionately. A single long-stemmed yellow rose lay trampled on the snow covered sidewalk, testimony to lost love and broken dreams.

She ran to the phone, not sure if she was going to scream at the top of her lungs or tell him she couldn't live without him. She stopped dialing before she got halfway through his number, needing to think it through. It would be rude not to call. But how could she call without giving in? Maybe she'd get his answering machine. That's it, she could call during the day tomorrow when she would be sure he was out of the house, either at Lucille's or in his studio. She'd call during her morning break. A coward's way out, but the best for both of them at any rate.

Conrad had sent the package by next day mail so he knew it had been delivered. The recording said a Kelsie Evers had signed for it. He waited by the phone for Samantha to call. How could she not call? At midnight he gave up and went to bed.

The next morning, no matter how hard he tried, he couldn't get around. His feet dragged and he made sure he stayed close to one of the phones. When it rang at 10:30, he pounced on it.

"Hello?"

"Oh...I was afraid you'd be out."

"No, I'm running a little late."

"Well...I wanted to call and thank you for the paintings."

"You're welcome."

"I was going to call last night, but..."

"But..."

"I'm sorry. I should have called. It was just that...well, I was feeling so fragile and I didn't know what to say."

"In other words, you were afraid you might get soft hearted and say what I'm waiting to hear. Right? So you figured at this time of the day I'd probably be either up in the studio or down at Lucile's and you'd get my machine. Right again?"

"Conrad, I..."

"Well, you've done your duty. Sorry I picked up and spoiled your game. Call again if you want. I promise I won't answer. I've got to get going. Maybe I'll talk to you later." He was gone and she felt like the low-life that she knew she was.

Chapter 7

Conrad closed the hatch to the attic. He didn't want the kids to know he was up here. They were downstairs with Ada making Christmas cookies. Fragments of Justin's uninterrupted sentences drifted up the stairs.

In a box shoved way in the back corner were the gifts Abby had been bringing home from Knoxville on that dreadful night. The garish Elvis TV trays for Jim's folks had been in the back seat and were crushed. The toys riding in the trunk were unharmed and Conrad wanted to see if there were any he could give the kids this year. He would wait until the time was right. Not on Christmas day, but maybe a few days before when a reminder of their parent's love would help ease the pain the holidays were sure to bring.

It hurt him to look at the toys Abby and Jim had picked out. There was a cloth book that was too young for Jessie now as she was well past the page-ripping stage. "Sorry, baby," he said silently as he set it to one side. Next he picked up a small box that held a tiny necklace with red rose buds painted on the mother of pearl pendant. This he set aside for Jessie. For Justin there was the

Power Ranger set that he had incessantly begged for. Conrad hadn't heard it mentioned lately and he decided against giving it to him. What if Justin realized that was one of the things his folks had gone to Knoxville for? Digging deeper into the box he found a child-sized wallet with western carvings of steer horns and horses. This would be Justin's present from Abby and Jim.

Along the side edge of the box was a flat package he hadn't noticed before. Opening it, he found a family portrait with four shining faces smiling up at him. They all looked so happy. Jim was looking at Abby instead of the camera. The love in his eyes made Conrad ache for Samantha as well as for his lost child. He sat holding the picture and the longer he thought, the more determined he became that he wasn't about to live without the love he could still have.

Did she love him? Of course she did. She had shown it in so many ways. He just had to find a way to convince her that he was the most important thing in the world to her. But how? He wasn't about to give up without a fight.

It had grown dark by the time Ada called to him from downstairs, telling him that supper was ready. His mind had been spinning a mile a minute and by the time he joined them he had a plan and a prayer.

"Can you stay and feed the kids, Ada?" he called out. "I've got some phone calls to make. Justin, Jessie, after supper we're going clothes shopping, so eat quick then get cleaned up. Lisa, you can wear that fancy dress we bought you for the Winterfest Dance." He stopped in his tracks, thinking on his feet. "Shoot, that's right, you're going to Florida with the Henson's day after tomorrow? Oh well, the three of us will have to do this by ourselves. Can you go shopping with us anyway? Okay then, everybody hurry and eat."

He grabbed the phone book to look up the number for United Airlines. As he dialed the toll-free number, his back was to the table and he missed the looks questioning his sanity that were passed along with the meatloaf around the kitchen table.

"Just don't say anything in your letters to Kelsie," he said over his shoulder seconds before the United operator picked up.

The reservations clerk laughed at him when he mentioned the date he wanted to fly but was fully recovered by the time she announced she had a three-seat cancellation that they could have. The price was ridiculous but that was the least of his worries.

"Hello, Ada? This is Samantha."

Ada smiled broadly, wiping her hands on the dishtowel. "Well, how good it is to hear from you. How are you, dear?"

"I'm doing okay. How about you?"

"Oh, I'm just fine." She waved Conrad and the kids out the door, not letting on that the phone call wasn't merely one of her friends from town wanting to yak for a while.

"I'm glad to hear you're feeling good. When I heard you had a lot of rain down there I got to thinking about your arthritis."

"Nope, everything is fine."

"Did Conrad show you the picture of my grand-daughter?"

"Why, yes and she sure is a little cutey."

"I know. I can't get enough of her. Um...is Conrad handy?"

"I'm so sorry Samantha, he just left. Him and the kids went shopping. He's really busy this time of year, you know, what with finishing stuff up for Christmas. I can have him call you later if you like. You know, when he has a minute to breathe."

She felt a little guilty, knowing that she wouldn't give Conrad the message at all. She'd let God take care of this little surprise by Himself.

"Okay, thanks. Merry Christmas to you and Carl."

"You too. And Samantha, I hope you have the best Christmas ever."

"Fat chance," Samantha replied gloomily as she hung up.

******

Chapter 8

Justin and Jessie stood in the downtown hotel room waiting for their final inspection. Conrad wished Lisa was here, for moral support if nothing else. But, of course, she had followed her already made plans to go to Florida. Never mind, he told himself. He'd manage this on his own.

He examined Justin first. His black suit coat was buttoned straight, the dark fabric contrasting sharply with his pale blond hair. Around his neck a red tie was decorated with tiny bright green Christmas trees. His pants had a sharp crease, as yet unwrinkled from sitting and squirming. Though he looked uncomfortable, Conrad knew he wouldn't complain.

Jessie twirled around watching her green jumper flare out from her red tights. The white lace-frilled blouse was attached to a thick petticoat that made the skirt stick out even when she wasn't spinning. Black patent leather shoes tapped out a tattoo on the tile floor of the entryway and she was enjoying the sound. Her sandy brown hair was tied away from her face in a big red bow. Justin had told her ever so solemnly that she looked exactly like a fairy princess.

When both kids passed his close examination, Conrad turned to the full length mirror on the wall near the door. He moved his hand down the smooth whiskers of his beard, glad he had taken the time to get it trimmed in the hotel barbershop last night. The string tie that wrapped snugly around his neck went well with his Western cut tuxedo. The coat hung past his knees in the back, somehow making him look taller. A gold embroidered satin vest was visible above the buttons.

Placing the black felt cowboy hat on his head, Conrad wondered if maybe this wasn't a bit of overkill. The saleswoman had sworn it made him look dashing, but then she was looking at a pretty good commission. Conrad was afraid it made him look a tad foolish. Oh well, Samantha had practically swooned over the hat he'd worn that night they took the sleigh to Ada's and that was his everyday hat. Besides, he could really use a good swoon about now.

Justin and Jessie stood in front of him, primping and making faces in the mirror. They all looked pretty darn good, if he did say so himself. How could she resist them?

"Grampy, are we gonna stand here all day or go find Sammy?" Justin impatiently tugged at his sleeve.

"Okay, okay. Showtime," Conrad said squaring his shoulders and taking a deep breath. He helped the kids with their coats, ignoring his for the sake of looking terrific.

Justin laughed. "Gee, Grampy, you'd think we was going to meet the President the way you're fussin'."

Jessie giggled and Conrad barely caught himself before mussing Justin's hair. Instead he led the kids to the waiting taxi.

The cab pulled up in front of the house that matched the address Conrad had for Samantha. Yes, this would be her house. The neighborhood wasn't the best in town but it was clean and pleasant and the small white-trimmed, mock-stone house fit her perfectly. He could picture her struggling in this bitter, unrelenting, ungodly cold to put up the live pine garland and tiny white lights that now hung across the front porch. Could picture her setting the antique sled and basket of pinecones near the door. Could picture her leaving it all to come be with him. Well, almost.

His hopes fell when he saw her car wasn't in the driveway. Instead, a black shiny sports car of some unknown variety was in its place. Please, God, let her be here...alone. He squared his shoulders and helped the kids up the slippery steps to the porch. An overgrown yellow dog barked ferociously then threw itself at the large window next to the door seconds after Conrad knocked. Justin and Jessie quickly slid behind Conrad's legs. Inside a man's voice told the dog to shut up and stay many times before he was finally able to open the door. The man, half Samantha's age, stood at the full glass storm door. He looked at the family on the porch as he tried to control the dog. Conrad started to speak.

"Dolly, will you shut up!"

"Hi, I'm Conrad Rich..." His voice was drowned out by the barking dog.

"Just a second. Let me put this wacky mutt in her pen. Come on, Dolly. Behave yourself for once, will ya."

He dragged the barking dog away from the door. When he came back a few seconds later he opened the door for them to come in. Jessie held back.

"Sorry about that but the dog goes ballistic every time somebody knocks. Sometimes I wonder why Mom puts up with her."

Conrad let out the breath he had been holding ever since he'd seen the sleek car. This was Jeff, Samantha's son. He propelled Justin through the door ahead of him and turned around to pick Jessie up in his arms.

"So you're Conrad, huh? Mom's told me all about you...well, maybe not all...but enough. I'm Jeff. Come on in."

The two men sized each other up as they stood in the living room of Samantha's house, Conrad feeling overdressed in his tuxedo and Jeff feeling underdressed in his U2 T-shirt and sweat pants. Minutes passed as they listened to the dog barking at the back of the house.

"Is she here?" Conrad finally asked.

"Uh, no. They took off for the holidays. Mom and Kelsie both."

Conrad felt his heart sink to his knees. No? Gone? For the holidays?

"I'm sorry. It was kind of a last minute trip, I guess. She called me up a couple of days ago and asked if I could come feed the dog. Said they'd been able to catch a last minute flight. Something about going away to get warm. We, Carrie and I, were pretty surprised that she would miss the baby's first Christmas and all."

Conrad tried to pull himself together enough to think of polite things to say. Finally something appropriate came to mind.
"Hey, congratulations on that baby girl of yours. Robyn Kay, right?"

"Yeah, how'd you know? Mom didn't tell me you and her were keeping in touch." Jeff eyed him warily.

"She sent me an announcement and we do talk on the phone every so often." Obviously not often enough, Conrad thought disgustedly. "She was bubbling with pride when she finally called a few days after Robyn was born. She wouldn't be gone over Christmas unless she really needed to get away." Conrad felt a pang of guilt. Had he driven her away from her family, made her crazy with his calls and his none to gentle pressure?

"Did she know you guys were coming? I mean, it seems like she would have mentioned it to me. You know, if a tall dark stranger in a tuxedo and a couple of really cute little kids come to the door, tell them I'll be back in a week or so. Something like that."

"No," Conrad sank uninvited into a chair. Jeff sat on the arm of the couch across from him. "I thought we'd surprise her. Looks like she got the last laugh on me, didn't she?" He stopped and ran his hand across his eyes. Fatigue from the rush of the past few days overwhelmed him suddenly and he felt as if a ton of bricks had been dumped in the seat of his pants. "Shit," he said softly.

"Grampy!" Justin had never ever heard that word come out of his Grampy's mouth, although he knew it from when Kevin Saunders got his mouth washed out on the first day of kindergarten.

Conrad opened his eyes and looked at Justin. "I'm sorry. I shouldn't have said that. Forgive me?"

Justin nodded his head.

"Nice puppy," Jessie's voice came from a distant room. Both men were instantly on their feet and running. They found Jessie standing near the pen where Dolly was wagging her tail ecstatically.

"She doesn't bite," Jeff explained. "She just gets overly rambunctious. I was afraid Dolly might nip her if she put her fingers in the pen. Here, stand back a minute and I'll let her out. Come on, Dolly, sit and let the nice little girl pet you."

Dolly sat, her whole body quivering with excitement. Jessie cautiously reached her hand out and laid it on Dolly's head. She stroked her nose and fingered the silky softness of her ears. Justin came up behind her and Dolly ceremoniously shook hands with him.

"Well, we better get out to the airport and let you get back to your family. Shoot, we let the cab leave. Can I use the phone?"

"You flew in just to see Mom? You must have just missed her at the airport. That's a shame. Well, I can take you out there on my way home. I live that direction anyway. Let me finish up with this nutty dog and we can go."

"I hate to put you out."

"No problem. Do you have a flight scheduled? It could be real difficult to get one, today especially."

"Yeah, I wasn't sure your Mom would be all that glad to see us so I booked a return flight, hoping I'd have to postpone it." He looked at his watch. "We'll have to wait for a couple of hours, but that's okay."

"Why don't you come have lunch with us. I'd like you to meet Carrie and Robyn Kay. Besides, maybe the kids can take a little nap and you won't have to fight with them in the airport. Come on, I'll give her a call and see if she wants me to pick up Taco Bell or something."

"I hate to put you out," Conrad said, hoping Jeff would insist.

"No problem. Besides, I heard we came really close to you being my dad. I'd like to find out what I missed."

Conrad felt his face flush with embarrassment. What exactly did Samantha tell you, his eyes asked Jeff. But Jeff only smiled then turned away to call his wife.

Chapter 9

Samantha stopped the rented Escort half way up the drive. How could she have ever left this place? Though the mud had dried, the brown earth still lacked the pristine beautifying whiteness of the snow. But this place shouted "home" to her and she wondered how she'd managed to ignore it before. The huge pine bough wreath they'd all gathered cones for hung invitingly in the peak over the entrance to the porch.

Gunning the motor, she tore up some gravel as she heeded the urge to hurry to Conrad's door.

"Mom, control yourself," Kelsie snickered as the car skidded to a stop.

Samantha glanced at her, making sure she was kidding instead of complaining. After setting the brake she jumped out of the car and bounded up the porch steps. She hopped from foot to foot as she waited at the door for Kelsie, running her fingers through her travel-mussed hair. Kelsie sauntered casually up behind her. "Settle down before you have a coronary or something."

Samantha drew a deep, calming breath down into her toes. Slowly she tried to exhale the tension. She succeeded a little but the anxiety was still there. What ifs filled her head. What if he didn't want her here anymore? What if she'd come all this way, wasted more of her rapidly dwindling savings, and he turned her away? What if..."

"Mom, would you like me to knock or are we going to let Santa deliver us with the toys?"

"All right. Okay. Give me a minute, will you? I'm a little nervous, in case you hadn't guessed."

"Oh yeah. I figured that when you ran that stop light back in Pigeon Forge. It's not going to get any easier. Knock!"

Samantha raised her knuckles and knocked softly on the door.

After waiting thirty seconds with no answer, Kelsie said, "Here, let me," and pounded hard enough to rattle the windows. The sound reverberated through the pines. Still no answer. They stood for a few minutes without saying a word.

Samantha checked her watch. It was almost 11:00.

"He might be up in his studio," she said, trying to keep the disappointment out of her voice. "I'll go check. You try the barn. Maybe they're out there feeding Petal."

"It's too quiet. Admit it, Mom. Nobody's home."

"Well, look anyway,"she said, more sharply than she had intended, before setting off up the mountainside. She didn't know what else to do.

Her black jeans and red and black checkered jacket soaked up the winter sun and warmed her as she huffed and puffed up the steep incline. Knowing the studio was never locked and after knocking briefly, she let herself in. It looked pretty much like it had when she had been here a month ago except for one major difference; there was a no work in progress. The work table didn't even have paper on it. A chair was pulled up to the window, and she could picture Conrad using the sill as a footrest as he often did in the house.

"Where are you? Did you run into town?" she asked the walls. "Will you be back by the time I get down the mountain?" She thought of the yellow satin gown wrinkling in her suitcase, the one she thought he'd never get to see. Maybe she'd been right about that after all. She should have listened to Kelsie when she told her to call ahead, but she couldn't risk him telling her that it didn't matter anymore.

She pulled the door shut quietly behind her. As she stepped out onto the porch, a squirrel's chatter broke the silence. She crossed over to the barrel, pulled out a handful of nuts.

"Tell me where he went and these are yours, Chucky."

He told her in no uncertain squirrel terms what he thought of her.

"Oh, never mind." She tossed the nuts across the porch and made her way down to Kelsie, who met her at the bottom of the path.

"Nobody's anywhere around. Now what?" Kelsie was dying to say, "I told you so" but knew that was the last thing she should bring up right now.

Now what? Good question.

"Let's leave a note on the door and go down to Ada's place. She'll know where they are. I'm sure they ran into town for a minute and they'll be back soon." Please, God, please, she silently added, keeping the prayer between God and herself.

They headed back down the winding driveway. After a few minutes on the road they stopped in front of a small, neat home. It looked different without the snow coating the yard but Samantha was sure this was the place.

She wasn't leery to knock on this door, knowing Ada would be glad to see her. No question about that. But when the door was opened, consternation was unmistakable in the older woman's eyes.

"Why, Samantha, what in the world are you doing here?" Her lack of warmth was apparent.

Samantha's spirit hit rock bottom. After everything else, to have this woman be unhappy to see her was almost more than she could bear. But then who could blame her. Ada had thought Samantha was different but in the end she'd hurt Conrad as bad or worse than Julia ever had.

Oh, why was everything going wrong?

"I'm really sorry to bother you, but..." Unshed tears sounded in her voice.

"For heaven sakes, nothing to be sorry about. You're no bother. Come in child. I was surprised to see you is all. Is that Kelsie in the car?" Standing in the doorway and motioning for Kelsie to come in, she obviously had recovered from whatever snit she had been in seconds ago.

"Carl, you remember Samantha don't you? Conrad's friend. And Kelsie. You met them in church that day. Remember?"

Carl had entered from the dining room, wiping his mouth discretely on a napkin. "Of course I do. I'm not senile yet."

"We've interrupted your lunch. I'm sorry, but I was wondering if you could tell me..."

"Don't you fret none about our lunch. We were just finishing up. Would you folks like a hot bowl of white bean chili and a slab of fresh-baked cornbread?"

Samantha shook her head.

"Kelsie? How 'bout you?"

Kelsie shot a quick look at her mother, then eagerly nodded. Ada linked an arm through Kelsie's and led her to the dining room.

Once they were sitting at the table with steaming bowls of chili, Samantha again tried to bring up the reason for her visit.

"Do you know where Conrad and the kids are? We were up to his place and there's no one around. We walked around for a bit but they didn't come home. Do you know if they ran up to Knoxville or something?"

"You know, it's the strangest thing. Conrad came to see me the other day. When was that, Carl? Tuesday or Wednesday?" Samantha caught a look between them.

"Wednesday, I guess. Anyway, he said he was going to take the kids away for a spell. Said it would be better than sitting around here waiting for Christmas to strike. That was his exact word...strike...like it was going to be some kind of a blow."

"Did he tell you where they were going?"

"No, I don't think he did say. Just away for a few days, t'was all. Until Christmas was over."

They ate silently for a while. Samantha stirred her chili and shredded the cornbread into tiny pieces. Deep in the agony of loneliness, she couldn't find the strength to pull herself out. If only she had called. Maybe then...

"How's he been? Are the kids okay?" She forced herself to make conversation.

"He sure was blue for a while after you left but lately he's been pretty chipper. Wednesday he was sounding better than he has in a long time." She gave this time to sink in before she added, "Didn't say why though, did he Carl?"

Carl frowned at his wife of fifty years, begging her not to make him an accomplice.

"No, I don't guess he said much to me about it," his scruples finally let him answer.

So. Conrad was adjusting. Not only to life without her but to life in general. Maybe he was finally finding his peace. Samantha wished she could be glad for him but it seemed to mean he didn't want her anymore and that caused the dull ache in her chest to return.

She pushed her chair back from the table and stood up. Kelsie looked at her over a raised soup spoon.

"Thanks. We'd better be going, Kelsie. Our flight leaves soon."

"But, Mom?"

"You flew all this way just to say hi?" Carl asked innocently.

"No. No...we were...uh...on our way to Florida and had a long layover in Knoxville so we thought we'd drive out and see how everyone was." Lies, lies, lies.

Ada knew for sure now that she wasn't the only one telling tales.

"I didn't know any airlines were using Knoxville as a stopover. Anyway, I'm right sorry you missed Conrad and the kids. They'll be disappointed."

Kelsie laid her spoon in her empty bowl and stood up. "Thanks for keeping her talking so I could finish my lunch. It was delicious."

"Thank you, child. You come by anytime." She beamed at Kelsie, liking the young woman and enjoying the thought of getting to know her better. She linked her arm through Samantha's and Kelsie's as they walked to the door. Carl brought up the rear.

"Maybe you shouldn't tell Conrad we were here. He might read more into it than he should."

"Nonsense. Conrad's a grown man. Besides he'll be glad to hear you stopped by. You come back when you can stay longer, okay?" Giving them each a quick peck on the cheek, she gently pushed them towards their car. "Drive careful now."

She stood beside Carl on the porch, waving them off.

"Why didn't you tell her where Conrad was? It would have made her so happy. Now she's leaving all broken hearted, thinking he doesn't care."

"That's between the two of them. I didn't say anything about him not wanting her. I only said he was happier. That was the God's honest truth. As soon as he decided to go after her he was a heck of a lot happier. Nervous as all get out, but happier. God'll get them together in His own sweet time. Maybe they need a chance to realize how important it is. Besides, it's not my business to tell her where he is."

Carl considered mentioning that it had never stopped her before but thought better of it. If he wanted a moment's peace this afternoon, he'd better keep his mouth shut.

"Come on, you old matchmaker. Time we finished up those cookies for the church." It was, far and away, the safest thing he could think of to say.

Chapter 10

Conrad gazed out the small window of the plane. Justin lay sound asleep in the seat next to him and Jessie was curled up snugly on his lap. He adjusted her head then absentmindedly straightened her dress so it wouldn't wrinkle. Looking at the pretty little party dress, he realized that it didn't matter now if it wrinkled or not. He was thankful he had bought round-trip tickets, or they be stranded in that God-forsaken iceberg of a place.

The person they had flown six hundred and some miles to impress was off gallivanting across the country. Someplace warmer was all Jeff could or would tell him. She had a lot of nerve not sitting home moping over him. Right now, while he sat in this stuffy 737, she was probably sunning herself on some Florida beach, or maybe even enjoying a drink with some guy, or maybe even... Jessie stirred in his lap. Her velvety dress was crushed tightly in his hand. He released his grip, brushed absently at the fabric then petted her hair as if she were a small kitten. She snuggled deeper into his chest and mumbled something about Muffin.

Dozing off to the thrum of the engines, he dreamed sad, frightening dreams. In one he stood on a sunny beach; tall, waving grasses lined one side, the ocean the other. Samantha waltzed in and out of the scene getting further and further away each time she reappeared. He ran toward her, trying to get closer, to call her back. Nothing helped. Soon she was only a mirage settling on the horizon. No, no! Please, God, don't take her away.

"I'm sorry sir, but the Captain announced it was time for seat belts." Jessie was being carefully wrenched from his arms. "We have to put her in the seat for her own protection. She'll be fine, won't you, honey?"

Conrad released his grip on a very confused Jessie. The stewardess locked her in her seat then smiled a forced smile at him before walking away.

"Jeez, Grampy. You acted like you was never gonna see her again or something. What a wacko."

Conrad gave Justin a shaky, embarrassed smile. "Sorry," he muttered as he regained control over his jittery emotions.

Samantha rubbed at her forehead trying to erase the throbbing ache battering her brain. They were on stand-by for a flight back to Michigan. Stand-by. On the day before Christmas that could mean anything from "we have room on the next flight" to "Happy New Year." And any destination from Fort Wayne to Detroit to Chicago. Right now she didn't care where she went, as long as it was some-where closer to home and out of this congested airport.

She dug down in her purse and came up with a bottle of aspirin. Grimacing at the taste, she washed four down with warm, flat Diet Pepsi. Five-thirty, she thought her watch said, although everything around her had evolved into one big blur.

She'd never get out of here in time to spend Christmas with Jeff and his new family. Of course she'd have to call them when and if she ever got back in town. She had been very mysterious about her quick departure. Now that would backfire and she would have to give embarrassing details to her even quicker return.

Kelsie tried to sleep in the chair next to her. They were certainly not made for sitting in for hours on end, let alone sleeping. Finally, she wadded up her sweatshirt into a rough pillow shape and lay down on the floor, covering herself up with her winter coat. Samantha looked around at others doing the same thing. Waiting, as she was, for a flight out of here.

Where had he gone? It had been a week since they'd talked and he hadn't said anything about any trips and she was sure he wouldn't be doing a lot of driving on Christmas Eve Day. She had been so sure he would be standing in the kitchen, starting a nice turkey dinner, doing everything in his power to keep the kids' minds away from the memories that couldn't be hidden. But she knew that he would be foolish and loving enough to try.

He should have come to the door in his "manly" apron and showered her with hugs and kisses. Especially kisses. Oh those heavenly kisses. She fanaticized momentarily about the feel of those lips then pulled herself back together. Had she moaned out loud? She glanced furtively at the old gentleman three seats away. He had his nose in a copy of "Newsweek" but a small smile crinkled the corners of his eyes.

She turned back to the book in her lap, not able to remember a word she had read this whole long, unending afternoon.

Had she blown it? Waited too long and tried too hard to dismiss what she felt for him? Been too convincing in her rejections of him and his life?

"Dammit, Samantha, you've done it now," she said to herself. "One good chance comes along and you mess it up. Will you never learn?"

"Mom!" Kelsie propped herself up on one elbow. "People will hear and think you've gone nutso."

"Was I..."

"Yes, Mom. Loud and clear." She rolled back over, giggling quietly into the sleeve of her coat.

"It's all right, dear." The man moved slowly to two seats away. "I don't think anyone but me heard you."

He whispered, but Kelsie turned over on her back with her eyes half opened, watching.

"I'm sorry I bothered you." Samantha tried to pretend great interest in her book so he would mind his own business. Out of the corner of her eye, she saw him smile and return to his own magazine.

She concentrated on keeping quiet. Soon exhaustion took over and she let her head rest on the back of the chair.

"Samantha Evers. Please come to the United Airlines Desk. Samantha Evers to the United Airlines Desk, please."

Samantha sat up straight, forced her aching body into an upright position and hurried over to the desk.

"I'm Samantha Evers. Please, please, please say you finally have a flight for us."

"You're in luck, Ms. Evers. We have a last minute cancellation on the next flight. It boards in ten minutes. Bring your luggage up and we'll put it through."

Samantha hurried back and nudged Kelsie's sleeping form with her foot.

"Come on, Kelsie. Wake up. We got a flight home. Hurry up now."

Kelsie sat up slowly and tried to focus on where she was. Oh yeah, airport. Forever! Home? Mom had said home. She bounded up and grabbed her suitcase as she ran to the desk.

"Come on, Mom."

Samantha smiled a wearily at her daughter as she followed her through the maze of last minute travelers.

Once their luggage was checked and their tickets updated they went to wait at the gate.

Chapter 11

A totally weary Conrad was dumbfounded that, even though Justin had gone to the bathroom three times on the plane, he still insisted that he had to go again once they landed. He hated taking Jessie into the Men's room, but knew from past experience that he had no choice.

Of course, once there Jessie had to go too. She still needed a little help with her tights and it was a snug fit in the tiny stall.

Everyone was tired and cranky and what at another time might have brought fits of laughter, today made them all the more irritated.

Conrad caught a glimpse of himself in the mirror as they walked to the door. He looked like hell. His tuxedo jacket was wrinkled, and dog hair clung to the seat of his pants. His hair was mussed from the high-backed seats on the plane.

"Who cares?" he asked the angry reflection before stuffing his slightly flattened cowboy hat on his head and exiting the bathroom.

"Carry me, Grampy," Jessie whined as soon as he pulled their baggage off the carousel. Conrad looked down as she tugged on his pant leg. He was already carrying two suitcases, their coats, Jessie's rag doll and Justin's bear. Justin had a firm hold on Jessie's hand close at Conrad's side.

"You'll have to walk, Jess. It's not far. Grampy has his hands full."

Jessie tugged her hand away from Justin and stopped walking. In the middle of the moving crowd she stood still, whining and rubbing her eyes sleepily.

Exasperated, Conrad switched both suitcases to one hand, threw the coats over his arm, and hurled Justin's bear at him. He picked Jessie up, none too gently, and thrust her doll into her arms. Her whining switched to whimpering then to full-fledged crying.

"Grampy, don't be so mean," Justin wailed. He looked at Conrad in amazement, then puckered up his face. Conrad hurried them to an uncrowded side hallway and sat Jessie down. Kneeling on his haunches, he pulled both kids close to him.

"I'm sorry, kids. Grampy's tired too."

"Okay."

"If we can make it to the car, we'll be all right. It's in the upper ramp so all we have to do now is ride up the escalator. That'll be fun, won't it? Then you can take a nap while Grampy drives home. We'll drive down through town and see the lights if you're awake by then."

"How come Sammy didn't come home with us?" Justin asked innocently, yet in his most exasperating tone.

"I told you, she wasn't there."

"But why didn't you call her and tell her we was coming?" Justin wanted to know. Again.

Conrad pinched the bridge of his nose between his forefinger and thumb. "We wanted to surprise her, remember?"

"Sure, Grampy. Some surprise."

"Never mind. For now let's figure out how we can get all this to the car. Justin, you take your bear, and your coat. Jessie, you take your doll and your coat. I'll carry the suitcases, my coat and Jessie. Justin, you'll have to stay real close to me so you don't get lost."

"I'm not a baby."

"I know but stay close, all right?"

They loaded up and headed to the escalator.

"Mom? I don't know how to tell you this, but I think I must have left my purse over where we were sitting. I can't find it anywhere."

"Oh, Kelsie. Run and get it. Hurry. For your sake I hope it's still there."

Samantha watched as Kelsie searched over and around the chairs. She turned to Samantha, shrugging her shoulders helplessly.

"We'll be right back," she said to the flight attendant over her shoulder as she dashed across the room. "Please don't let them leave without us," she begged.

"I've looked everywhere, Mom. I don't know where it could be." Kelsie's eyes clouded over. She looked like a small dejected child.

"Where did you have it last?"

"I don't know. I can't remember. I'm so tired."

"Think, Kelsie, think."

"I...I had it when I bought the magazine in gift shop."

They flew across the heavy foot traffic and into the store. Kelsie described her purse to the young man behind the counter.

"This it?" he asked, smiling and holding up a small black bag. "I just got here and I haven't had time yet to check the identification or call anyone about it yet."

"Yes! Thanks, oh thanks a lot." Kelsie recovered quickly from her panic and exhaustion. She was enjoying the admiring looks this handsome young man was throwing her way.

"Come on, Evers, we've gotta catch that flight. Let's go."

"One second, Mom, I have to let him photocopy my I.D. in case there's a problem later. Don't I?" She nodded her head enthusiastically at the smiling young man, hoping the message had gotten through.

"Yeah, store policy. Sorry but I'll be right back."

Samantha glared at her. "Kelsie Marie, if we miss this flight..." She let the rest of the sentence hang as she walked out of the store, and waited impatiently at the entrance.

Chapter 12

"Where we gonna eat, Grampy? I'm hungry."

"Me too, Grampy. Me too."

Samantha knew she was hallucinating when she heard Justin's voice calling out to his Grampy. It couldn't be him. A man's elbow jammed her ribs as he hurried past.

"Excuse me," he flung over his shoulder, not really looking at her, his mind and eyes on the door many yards ahead. A black cowboy hat shielded most of his face, but somehow he looked familiar. Heartrendingly familiar.

The man stopped dead in his tracks. People crashed into him from behind, glaring and cussing as they detoured. He turned back to the woman he had almost knocked down. It was her. Incredible as it was, Samantha stood only a few yards away, staring at him. Justin stopped a few feet beyond him and followed his gaze.

"Samantha!" he shouted loud enough to drown out the page for last call on United Air Flight 217.

The three of them struggled to make their way up the downstream flow of people. Samantha waited anxiously at the storefront, unable to trust her legs as they wobbled beneath her.

"What are you doing here?" Conrad asked when he finally stood beside her. Her face was puffy, her eyes red, and her hair stuck out at weird angles. Yet no one ever looked better to him in his whole life.

"I came to see you. What on earth are you doing here?" she asked, looking down and up at the rumpled tuxedo and the slightly off kilter hat.

"We just got off a flight from Michigan. Where we went to see you."

"You what?"

Conrad's grin horizontally split his face. She had come to him. She wouldn't do that unless she meant to stay. Would she? Slowly he sat the luggage and coats down. He took Jessie's doll and laid it on the suitcase. Taking Justin's bear and jacket, he laid them down too.

Kelsie deserted her new-found friend, and hurried over to see what was going on.

Standing Jessie on her feet, Conrad looked nervously at the crowd of people around him then removed his hat and put it over his heart. He whispered, "Ready, guys?"

They formed a line in front of Samantha. Conrad went down on one knee. Justin joined him, switching knees to match Conrad. Jessie tried to curtesy, stumbled, then joined them on bended knee.

"That's okay, honey," Conrad said, unable to keep the shake out of his voice. "Ready?" He looked at both of them as they nodded; tired bodies and growling stomachs forgotten as they repeated what they had rehearsed in the motel the night before. People stopped and stared at the impromptu entertainment. Conrad swallowed hard.

"Samantha, I love you more than life itself. Will you marry me?"

"Yeah, Sammy, will you marry us?"

"Please, Sammy. Marry us?"

There was not a two second gap between question and answer.

"Yes," she exhaled as if her entire life had been hinging on those words.

Conrad's face turned pasty. Did she say yes?

Samantha knelt beside them on the floor.

"Yes," she said to Conrad alone, holding his cheeks between her hands and looking deep into his eyes. Then she turned to Justin and Jessie and said yes to each of them.

The paleness left Conrad's face as he hauled himself and her up to kissing position. Smiling faces watched as he pulled her into his arms, kissing her soundly to impress no one but himself. Soon he forgot the crowded airport as he fell deeper and deeper into the kiss.

"My turn, my turn. Don't be such a hog, Grampy."

With all of the hugs, kisses and excited chatter, none of them heard the page for Samantha Evers to report to the United Airlines desk. It would be hours before any of them thought of their luggage, now heading North without them.

PART

THREE

The tourists were missing on Gatlinburg's main street. They'd all gone home to their families and loved ones. The shops were closed and only the front window decorations were lit. The people wandering the streets on this warmer than normal Christmas Eve were locals, and Conrad spoke briefly to many of them. He carried Jessie on one arm and securely hung on to Samantha's hand with his free hand. Justin gripped her other hand, swinging it back and forth, making wide arcs.

Kelsie walked a little ways ahead. Two of the teenage boys Lisa had introduced her to at church stopped to talk, then fell in with her as she examined the shop windows. She timidly tried the flirting smile that had worked so well at the airport.

Conrad and Samantha watched her, both a little wary of the young lady she was becoming and the trials they would soon have to face.

But for now, Samantha was happy just to be beside Conrad and couldn't keep her mind off the fact that he was going to be hers for the rest of her life. Laying her head on his shoulder, she raised her left hand. Since it was tightly entrenched in Conrad's, she raised his at the same time. The emerald cut diamond twinkled brightly under the lights, picking up the red and green from the wreath overhead and reflecting it back. She was the luckiest woman alive.

Conrad watched her, enjoying her reaction to the ring's sparkle. It had taken him and the kids more time to pick out than all their clothes put together.

Justin tugged sharply on Samantha's other hand.

"Come here, Sammy. I want to show you something." He started to pull her. "No Grampy, I only want Sammy."

Conrad let go and watched them curiously as they walked up to the big window in the Gatlinburg Drug Store. Strictly business, even in the Christmas season, it was full of crutches, walkers and other various hospital equipment. What on earth?

Samantha kneeled down to see what had attracted Justin.

"Everybody's trying real hard to pretend I don't know what tonight is," he confided as he stared at the crutches laying on their sides behind the window. "But I do. I remember this is the night Mommy and Daddy went to heaven."

Samantha pulled him away from the window and into her arms. He came easily and cried long and hard on her shoulder. She saw Conrad start to move towards them, and waved him away. Jessie curled up in Conrad's arms and somberly watched Justin cry. Up ahead Kelsie ditched the boys and headed back. They all stood a few feet away and watched Samantha and Justin.

Her leg muscles screamed to be out of this cumbersome position but she held him steadily, gently rocking him from side to side. After many minutes Justin raised his head and rubbed his eyes with the back of his fists.

"I know Mommy and Daddy sent you to us. Them and God. Sammy, I'm real glad you're here. You too, Kelsie. I think Mommy and Daddy brought you down here from that awful, cold place to help Grampy and Lisy and us. And we, Jessie and me, we was wondering if maybe we could start calling you Grammy a week early."

Samantha looked into Justin's eyes. Even if the powers that be had allowed her to leave Conrad for good, how could she ever have let go of the love of this little guy? She made sure her eyes said she was completely serious before she answered.

"That would be the best Christmas present in the whole wide world."

A slow grin replaced the frown on Justin's face. He let go of his hold on Samantha and ran over to Conrad. "See Jessie, I told you it'd be okay, didn't I? Hey, it makes a rhyme. Grammy Sammy."

"Grammy Sammy, Grammy Sammy," the two children chanted over and over while Samantha tried in vain to pull her resisting body upright. Conrad ambled over and offered her his hand. She looked at it, took it and let him help her get the kinks straightened out as she slowly stood up.

Christmas carolers strolled up behind them singing "Oh Holy Night." The group was from Conrad's church and many of the faces looked vaguely familiar to Samantha. She recognized Reverend Hulburt as he beamed expectantly while they finished the song.

"Conrad. Samantha," he said gravely when he was able to speak. "Something to tell us on this holiest of nights?"

Conrad held up Samantha's ringed hand for the Reverend's benefit. The crowd around him oohed and ahhed in appreciation.

"We were going to ask you in church tomorrow morning, but now's as good of time as any. Will you be able to marry Samantha and me on New Year's Eve? We were hoping for a midnight service."

"I'd be right honored to join the two of you. We were praying for this, you know. New Year's Eve, huh?"

Beside them Reverend Hulbert's wife, Bernice, laughed.

"Gale hasn't seen midnight in so many years, I doubt if he could hold his eyes open that long. But if you're serious, I'll see to it that he takes a long nap after the football game."

After congratulations were passed and slaps on the back were exchanged, the group wandered away singing "Go Tell It On the Mountain", some of them glancing back and grinning before they turned the corner.

"Too late to back out now," Conrad said when they were gone. He looked down into her eyes, finding none of the reservations he had seen so many times before. He pulled her close, turning slightly sideways to make room for Jessie. Her lips on his told him all he needed to know, though she never said a word.

"Let's go see if the ducks are in the river," Kelsie said to Justin. He impatiently waited for Conrad to let Jessie down, then grabbed her hand as the three of them hurried over to the water. "Don't worry, Da...Conrad," Kelsie shouted over her shoulder. "We'll catch up with you in a few minutes."

Conrad and Samantha stopped to look in some store windows as they made their way down the street, knowing that neither one would remember the next morning what they had seen.

When they reached the well lit archway that ran along the river, Conrad pulled her aside. The white lights reflected in their eyes as they looked solemnly at each other.

"Love you," he whispered gently, his lips against her forehead. It had to be the fiftieth time he'd said it in the last three hours.

"And I love you," she answered for at least the forty-ninth time. "You know, I thought I knew what I wanted from this life. I knew where I was headed and exactly how I was going to get there. I thought I wanted to be on my own, beholden to no one. But I was wrong. All I ever needed was waiting for me right here. Under these Gatlinburg lights."

"I know, Darlin'. Let's round up the kids and go home."

"Home," she whispered in answer. Her thoughts as they listened to the children chatter on the way back to the van were not on the horrible florescent kitchen paint that would take at least four coats to cover, or on the tacky gray linoleum that would have to be painstakingly scraped up before getting down to that marvelous oak floor. Not even the red metal paint for the roof could invade her mind tonight.

No, tonight her mind was on tucking Justin and Jessie in bed. And on saying goodnight to the Kelsie, who would be sleeping on the couch. And on spending the first of what she hoped to be at least one hundred Christmas Eves wrapped in Conrad's artistic arms.

The lights twinkled all around her; their glowing warmth radiantly watching over her, this man she loved and the family that was hers and his, now and forever.

Her eyes rose to the pinpricks of light from the mountains encircling them. As always, it started with the mountains. Finally, after years of wandering and wondering, she knew why.

The end or the beginning;
it's all relative.

A NOTE FROM THE AUTHOR

I hope you have enjoyed *Gatlinburg Lights*. Writing it has been a labor of love that has brought about some major changes in my life. Or maybe I should say, gave me the courage to do what I've always wanted to do...move to the Smoky Mountains. I love my life here and try to spend every possible moment traveling the backroads in the Park and out in surrounding areas. I can even call it research so I'm working while I wander. What a deal!

My next three books will be seasonal renditions of love stories placed in these mountains. In each, I will highlight a different area of the Smokies and a different problem facing not-so-young-and-gorgeous women of today. I hope to have my second book, *Redbuds in the Smoke*, out in Spring of 1998. Please watch for it in area stores when you come to see how many wonderful shades of spring green and vibrant purple these mountains can portray.

Or write to me at the address on the order form on the next page.

Your friend in the Smokies,

Donna Lea